THE GREEK MYSTERIES

INSTITUTE OF RELIGIOUS ICONOGRAPHY
STATE UNIVERSITY GRONINGEN

ICONOGRAPHY OF RELIGIONS

EDITED BY

Th. P. van Baaren, L. Leertouwer, F. Leemhuis and H. Buning (*Secretary*)

SECTION XVII: GREECE AND ROME

FASCICLE THREE

LEIDEN
E. J. BRILL
1976

THE GREEK MYSTERIES

BY

UGO BIANCHI

With 48 plates

LEIDEN
E. J. BRILL
1976

ISBN 90 04 04486 8

PRINTED IN THE NETHERLANDS

CONTENTS

Introduction   I

Legends to the Illustrations   16

Illustrations . . . . at the end of the fascicule

INTRODUCTION

The 'Mysteries'

One must reluctantly admit that a treatise on the iconography of the Greek 'Mystery' religions is, because of their very nature, impossible. In fact, the secret of the Greek Mystery rites is always substantially respected in the literary sources available to us, and it was even more closely guarded in iconographical sources. This is in spite of the fact that various Eleusinian subjects frequently appear in ceramics, especially in those of Attic origin, as well as in other forms of figurative art, particularly in bas-reliefs.

What we have said about Eleusis is true also of those rites which the Greeks considered to belong to the same or to a similar category, even if they differed in some particular respect. We are referring to the Mysteries of Samothrace, or to the rites of other islands of the Thracian sea, sacred to the 'great gods', sometimes called *Kabeiroi* (Kabiri), whose mysterious rites were also celebrated at a special centre in Thebes devoted to the worship of Dionysos Kabiros. On the other hand, a special problem is presented by that particular current of religiosity of an esoteric and initiatory type which goes by the name of Orphism. This first appears to us in the Athens of the sixth century B.C., but found a fertile ground for expansion in Magna Graecia and Sicily, an expansion parallel to that of the Pythagorean Schools and spirituality, which had absorbed many specific characteristics of Orphism.

Still more complex are the problems connected with the worship of Dionysos, which seems to have at first displayed a more generically exoteric character, differing in this from Mystery cults like those of Eleusis or Samothrace, or mysteriosophic cults like Orphism: we shall return to these distinctions later. In any case the Dionysos cult also must be included in the whole question of the Mysteries, if for no other reason than because in the ages after Alexander it was more clearly recognised as a cult, or as a source of cults, of a 'Mystery' or even mysteriosophic type. There is also the fact, of enormous historical and religious significance, that Dionysos was an essential component not only of authentic Mystery rites, as in the above-mentioned case of the Kabirion of Thebes, but also of the Orphic type of spirituality. As regards the connection between the Dionysiac religion, or at least between Dionysos himself, and Eleusis, these constitute a separate problem which concerns the very nature and history of Eleusinian worship and the very concept of a 'Mystery' religion.

The Gods of the Mysteries

We must add, with reference to the Greeks' awareness of a particular typology to which all the elements of Mystery religions belonged, that the ancient writers, especially those most given to theological speculation like Plutarch, were well aware of the fact that the gods of the Mystery, myths and associated cults, were very different from the other gods, and in some way constituted a category apart in the varied world of the Greek pantheon. This is true not only of personages who were superhuman, mysterious and inaccessible by definition, like the 'great gods' and the Kabiri, who in their very name represent a separate category, but also of figures familiar and central in every Greek pantheon, deities like Dionysos and Demeter, and the latter's daughter, Kore-Persephone. This specific character of Dionysos and Demeter seems to have been clear to the Greeks from earliest times. Dionysos, whatever may have been his historical origin and the development of his story in Greek territory, was in a sense a stranger god among the Olympians. A whole section of Greek literature, the Homeric poems, hardly refers to him at all—but this does not mean that he was a 'recent' god. Demeter was ignored as well in those poems.

If we pass from arguments based on absence of references, arguments perfectly valid in this case even if the reasons for the silence are various, to explicit and positive testimonies, we must once more return to the theologian of Chaeronea, Plutarch. He refers to the peculiar character of Demeter and Dionysos in order to expound, on Platonic lines, a special theory he had about the categories of divine beings, whom he divides into two groups, gods and daemons.[1] Whereas the former are not subject to any mutation or development, thus showing that they belong to the Platonic category of the 'identical' or immutable (i.e. the 'divine'), the daemons instead suffer mutation and vicissitudes. Such are, according to Plutarch, Demeter and Dionysos, for their myths describe vicissitudes and sufferings which could not be attributed to beings fully endowed with the divine nature. He adds that superhuman beings like the Titans and the Giants, who belong to other categories and whose painful vicissitudes are narrated in mythology, are also daemons (and it is true that 'Titanic' characters may be recognised in those categories of 'mysteric' gods, to which Telchines, Kabiri, Kuretes—mythic initiators—as well, probably, as the Titans of Delphic legend did belong). To complete the picture, the sage of Chaeronea adds that Isis and Osiris (in his own language: Demeter and Dionysos), although daemons, finally acquired a full divine nature, becoming no longer daemons but gods. This gives them their proper place in the front rank of their respective mythologies, while at the same time preserving, by reference to their different characteristics, their nature as gods subject to mutability, that is, 'Mystery' gods.

In fact, this category of gods 'subject to change' is that which best befits personages like the two Eleusinian goddesses (Demeter and her daughter Kore-Persephone) and Dionysos and also, in so far as we can tell, the gods of Samothrace. Naturally we must always bear in mind, particularly as regards Demeter, Kore and Dionysos, those aspects which belong to myths and rites of a Mystery nature. This leads us from the nature of the Mystery god to the nature of the Mystery itself, as a mythical-ritualistic complex with its own peculiar characteristics. At the same time, the story of the god, and the nature of the mythical-ritualistic Mystery itself, allow to get an insight into the meaning and consequences of initiation, by means of which the neophyte acquires privileges and is promised happiness in this life and in the life after death.

The mythic-ritualistic complex of the Mystery religions

As we have already said, the Mystery cults, that is, those mythic-ritualistic manifestations which the ancients generally grouped together as mysteric (Mysteries) or even, less specifically, as *teletai* (Mystery rites), or even at times 'orgia' (rituals, often of a mysteric type), are peculiar to the Greek world. We have no reason for transposing them to other cultural regions, not even to the Egyptian world, although, as we have hinted at, this

---

[1] *De Iside*, 25; cf. *De E ap. Delphos*, 9.

included a large number of analogies, acknowledged by the Greeks themselves, with Greek ritual practices and mysteric gods.

In spite of these specific peculiarities of the Greek Mystery phenomena, religious historians and ethnologists have not hesitated to assimilate the Greek Mysteries with mythical-ritualistic manifestations far removed from them in time and space, and in their respective historical-cultural situations, like the initiatory rites of illiterate peoples. Such are the puberal rites of the tribes of south eastern Australia, studied at the end of the 19th century by Howitt and others (and, on a comparative basis, by Tylor and Lang). These rites are still grouped, for example by Elkin, under the conventional name of 'Mysteries'. Comparisons are also made with more complex initiatory societies, of a somewhat different type. For instance, the German ethnologist Jensen's researches into the beliefs of primitive agriculturalists, which he includes in a more comprehensive 'lunar' culture (the cultural cycle Frobenius called 'Malay-Nigritic'), have induced some classical scholars like K. Kerényi to suggest a typological affinity, or even a remote historical continuity, between the Eleusinian manifestations and the primitive myths in question. These contain an initiatory, chthonic and 'Mystery' element, centred in a story about a god(dess), closely connected with the evolution of agriculture and the destinies of man, to be fulfilled through and beyond death. Perhaps historical-religious comparative studies permit us to attempt—not without historical-cultural methodic reservation—what Greek sources do not permit, that is, to *begin* to 'localise' the essence and to surmise, if not properly to penetrate, some implications of the Eleusinian, Samothracian and Kabirian Mysteries. This because, unlike the Greek Mysteries, those of Australia, Melanesia, Africa and America, etc. have been wholly or partly profaned.

'Rites de passage', initiations, Mysteries

Let us now attempt to define the typology of the Greek mythical-ritualistic manifestations which we call 'Mystery' religions: in Greek, in the plural, *mysteria*. These manifestations are, as we have already said, peculiar, as far as our knowledge goes, to the Greek world; they must nevertheless be studied, in order at least to distinguish their special characteristics, against the background of a vaster typological complex, well known to religious historians: the so-called 'rites de passage' and 'initiations'.

The 'rites de passage', according to the terminology introduced in a famous book by Van Gennep, are, in fact, those rites which bring about and confirm the passage from one human status to another, from one condition to another which is socially defined, proclaimed, confirmed and guaranteed. This concept is very general, and its practical validity is sometimes contested by students of the comparative history of religions, but in our opinion it is perfectly valid and clearly defined in its typology and fundamental application. In practice it is realised in three phases or 'moments' in which the passage or transit takes place and is celebrated: there is a first moment of separation from a given preceding status, condition or group (or from the indistinguishable and undefined mass); then comes a second moment, a 'marginal' or intermediary state, in which the candidate no longer belongs to his former condition but does not yet belong to the new: therefore a temporary, anonymous painful and exceptional condition, marked by many tests and ordeals. In this state he is effectively separated from his preceding condition, although he has not yet been able to adhere to the new. Finally, there is a third phase, of aggregation, or attainment of the new status.

This concept of the 'rite de passage' is in its schematic simplicity very widely diffused in the world of religions (and in general in the world of social institutions and symbology) and characterised occasionally by actual transitions or passages even of a material nature, actions intended to signify, or even in some way to bring about, the above-mentioned change of condition. These 'passages' sometimes represent a new birth, on the very threshold of life (or simulation of new birth) or on the threshold of death (a symbolic entombment followed by a 'return to life' or better by a 'new birth'). The most general typology of the 'rite de passage' enables it to include a) those 'rites de passage' relating to the common (but always well defined in a historical and cultural context) cycle of existence (rites celebrating such 'passages' as birth, marriage and death—this last also being a passage which must be ritually confirmed and represented) and b) the rites of accession to a new status which implies adhesion to a clearly defined group: that is, initiatory rites in a more restricted sense.

The Mysteries of fertility and life

The study of the typology of 'rites de passage', and particularly of initiatory associations and rites, in order to obtain a better understanding of the various aspects of the Greek initiation rituals called Mysteries implies no diminution of our initial and still valid insistence of the unique character of the Greek Mysteries. This reservation is moreover strengthened by the fact that a line of somewhat different research is now necessary on the historical-comparative plane: we refer to the connection between the Greek Mysteries, particularly those of Eleusis, and the so-called 'fertility' rites of the regions of the Near East, rites which are present even in the pre-history of most of those mythical-ritual manifestations, also of Oriental origin, which are commonly included in the category of Mysteries and which belong to the Hellenistic-Roman Age (Mysteries of Attis, Adonis, Osiris and Mithras).

The question of the possible initiatory and Mystery character of the fertility rites of the Near East in archaic times, independently of the influence of Greek cults, is very obscure; we shall not deal with it here, although the Osirian rites in Egypt and the particular role of the king in the Tammuz rites of ancient Mesopotamia—apart from other examples—may seem to indicate the celebration of a secret rite of a seasonal character for the purpose of land's fertility: and an element of such a rite was certainly the mystic marriage of the king with the 'great goddess'. This is confirmed by a well known Assyrian document, of a later age (see Ebeling: 'Tod und Leben', No. 1) which assures the king of special personal blessedness in the Nether World because he has devoutly celebrated the New Year Festival. But we have no proofs of initiatory rites comparable to those described by Apuleius for Hellenistic-Roman Osiris religion.

Taking as our point of reference the Eleusinian Mysteries we may define this typical phenomenon of the Greek spirit as follows: *a mythical-ritual complex, implying an annual festival not without connection with the theme of seasonal fertility and the welfare of the city, but including very prominently the individual initiation of groups of citizens, and later on of men and women from all over the Greek and Hellenistic-Roman world. This initiation—protected by secrecy—conferred special personal privileges already in this life, but particularly in the afterlife.* Therefore here we have a collective intention, shared by all the citizens, associated with the seasonal renewal of the earth's fertility by means of a mystic marriage of the goddess and (probably) within the wider context of the introduction of cereal cultivation, symbolised by the sending of the hero Triptolemos throughout the world to teach the art of the new cereal agriculture. We have also an individual intention (closely connected with the collective intention): in fact, 'those who have seen these things' are proclaimed 'thrice blessed' ' (as Sophocles informs us in a well known fragment [2] referring to an Eleusinian ritual formula).

But the above given definition of the Eleusinian type of Mystery, although comprehensive, is incomplete because it lacks any reference (and such a reference is essential) to the deities of the Mysteries, the 'two goddesses', Demeter and her daughter Kore-Persephone, and to the relative myths, to the *hieros logos*, the sacred story which forms the aetiological basis of the Mysteries themselves. This reference to the gods and myths is essential, both as regards the collective character and intention of the Mysteries which is shared by all the citizens, and also as regards the individual intentions, the quest for prosperity in this life and in the life to come for every one of the initiates. As we have already said, the gods of the Mysteries are gods subject to vicissitude. They are subjects and objects of a series of vicissitudes which causes painful events like 'death' or loss to be followed by happy events like renewal of life and re-discovery of the lost. In the case of Eleusis (to which special importance is attached in this connection also because the myths of Samothrace are very little known) these events concern both the great goddesses. First we have Demeter the mother, whom we see deprived of her daughter and therefore disassociating herself from the Gods to whom she attributes the blame and dwelling among men as a mourner. On earth the goddess wishes to immortalise the boy Demophoon, the son of Celeus, King of Eleusis, but her attempt fails through the fault of the boy's mother, Metanira, who breaks the spell while the divine nurse is exposing the child to the immortalising flame. The king, nevertheless, obeys the goddess's command to found a temple in her honour. Finally, following the intervention of Zeus who assures the goddess that she will recover her daughter, things take a turn for the better. Demeter institutes the Eleusinian shrine and its Mysteries, which will bestow on the initiates certain privileges. These are not exceptional and decidedly super-human, as would have been the immortality for Demophoon, but a blessed destiny in the afterlife and happiness here on earth (associated with the welfare of the city and of its king). In the end Persephone returns but, magically bound to the other world by her ravisher and husband Pluton, who makes her Queen of the Infernal Regions, she will dwell annually with the gods on Olympus (and of course also in the Eleusinian shrine) for only two-thirds of the year. The other third she will spend in the nether world. Whatever the more immediate interpretations of this story may be, we see an obvious connection with the seasonal life of corn.

This divine narrative is also the basic reason for the initiate's bliss; it presupposes in fact that he takes part, in a symbolical but effective way, in the adventures of the two goddesses. He is present at the ritual, or rather he is an actor, during the celebrations at the shrine, in the great autumn initiation ceremonies. We cannot say that the initiate is in any way assumed into the divine nature, as bridegroom or son of one or other of the goddesses (or as a mystic father of the new born divine child whose birth—as it seems—is announced at

---

[2] Frg. 753 N[2] ; cf. *Hom. Hymn. Cerer.* 479-481. Pind. frg. 137 Schr.

every celebration) for we find no indication of this in any of the few sources available to us. But his participation in the adventures of the goddess, through 'vision' and 'sympathy', in the etymological sense of the term, implies a familiarity with these events which is enough to ensure for him a different fate, in the Nether World, from that of those who have not 'seen'. 'For him alone there will be life, down there', while for others 'everything down there will be evil' says the above quoted sophoclean fragment.

It is clear that the Eleusinian 'Paradise' is in the Underworld, in accordance with the general chthonic character of the two goddesses, which does not conflict with their Olympian nature (after all, Pluton is a brother of Zeus) and in accordance also with the link between the Eleusinian ritual and the great fertility cycle. With regard to the story of the two goddesses, although on the one hand their diverse roles make them different characters, endowing Demeter with a stability denied to her daughter who is bound to spend part of the year in Pluton's realm, yet it is no less true that both are re-established in their sovereign state as Olympic deities, enthroned in unchanging and eternal calm. This is because the story concludes or, at least as far as regards Persephone, is perpetuated cyclically, in a general state of permanence. It is this permanent though alternating stability which presides over the ordering and functioning of the cosmos, and causes the alternations of the seasons, due to the presence and (equally regular and, in effect, beneficial) absence of the daughter goddess. As we have seen, Plutarch, with an understanding worthy of a religious 'phenomenologist', penetrated very well this ambivalence intrinsic to the Demetriac mythology, interpreting it by recurs to the Platonic notion of gods and daemons.

Mystery knowledge and Mysteriosophy

But the Greek Mysteries, and in particular those of Eleusis, certainly contain an even more closely guarded secret, and one which is much more interesting than the veiled *hiera* (sacred objects), revealed by the hierophants on the occasion of the second and final initiation, that reserved to the *epoptai*, 'those who have seen'. We would like to know if and when the Eleusinian Mysteries, apart from the mystic 'seeing' which assured the initiates of their future destiny, on the strength of their familiarisation with the story of the goddesses, also contemplated an authentic 'mysteriosophy'. By this term we mean a special manner of seeing the cosmos, man and the history of the gods: a manner which implies a *sophia* or general mystic conception of life and of the cosmos, of its divine origins, of the perpetual and recurring cycle of changes which govern it, and also and in particular a doctrine of the soul as subject to an alternation of decay in this world subject to destiny (or to matter) and of final re-integration, or at least of final integration in the divine world—under the image of the concept of *soma-sema*, the body-tomb.

Typically 'mysteriosophic' is, in this connection, the whole complex of mythical-doctrinal notions generally known under the name of 'Orphism', from which are derived philosophical and para-philosophical interpretations like those of Empedocles, Pythagoras, to some extent Plato himself, Plutarch and, later on, the neo-Orphic, neo-Pythagorean and neo-Platonic Schools. Moreover, that speculations of this type were associated with an interest in the greatest shrines of Greece is clear to whoever reads Plato or, for example, Plutarch's short treatise on the E of Delphi.

Now the question is to know, in fact, whether and when the whole complex of Eleusinian mythical-ritual manifestations may have been enriched from within—and not merely exploited from without—by similar mysteriosophic notions. We would like to know whether these remained extraneous to the Mysteries, as such, and merely the object of Orphic speculations and utilisations similar in this respect to the speculations of the Gnostics above the doctrines of the Christian Church, speculations which were quite extraneous to the Christian traditions. We would also wish to know whether, eventually, Orphic (i.e. mysteriosophic) ideology became, even if not officially, an implicit part of the spirituality of Eleusis (as it happened with the 'Orphic' *lamellae* of Magna Graecia, for which see below), and was admitted as the explanation of that vicissitude of the goddess(es) which was commemorated in the autumn ceremonies of the shrine. [3]

The progress of an evolution: from the Mysteries to the Mysteriosophy

On the basis of our present knowledge the problem of the possible mysteriosophic content of the Eleusinian Mysteries must be considered insoluble, and so we must distinguish clearly between the two manifestations: a) one which is truly '*mysteric*', relating to the *mysteria* (mystery-religions), among which, e.g., are the typical rites and myths of the Eleusinian religion attested by archaeological and literary sources and b) the other which is 'mysterio-sophic', Orphic, rather than properly Eleusinian.

There is, however, another problem which must be solved, however difficult it may seem; the problem of the role of Dionysos in the context of the Eleusinian religion and of the time of his first appearance in this religion, probably when it was already formed and institutionalised. The hypotheses of the scholars vary very much about this. There are those who see Dionysos as a present and determining factor even in the earliest age of the Eleusinian cult (if not in the Eleusinian myth) and others who believe that he was introduced later, even relatively much later, in the IVth century B.C. Moreover, most scholars consider that his identification with Iacchus, or at least the aggregation of Dionysos to the Eleusinian world of which Iacchus was an integrating part (he was the spirit who led to the shrine the procession of candidates for initiation) is merely a secondary factor. Nor, according to these, did Iacchus, at least originally, have Dionysiac characteristics and implications.

As to whether Dionysos originally belonged to the Eleusinian religion, still less significance should be attached to a certain tendency, present in very ancient times, to associate Dionysos with Plutos, the god or genius of wealth, especially the fruits of the earth. This Plutos, in spite of being frequently represented as a child, seems more probably to have been an emanation or an aspect of the mythical and cult figure of Pluton, the husband of Persephone and chthonic giver of wealth. The horn of abundance, in spite of all possible original or acquired connections with Dionysos, belongs in the Eleusinian world to Plutos as well as to Pluton.

As we have said, the problem of the presence of Dionysos in the Eleusinian religion, and of his questionable antiquity, must not be confused with an even greater problem we have already referred to: we mean the question of Orphic and mysteriosophic elements in the theology of the Eleusinian Mysteries. In fact we must distinguish the Orphic Dionysos, integrated in a mysteriosophic context, from all the other figures of Dionysos occurring in Greek myths and cults.

---

[3] What is that *penthos*, that 'grief', of Persephone for which men pay a ransom according to Pindar άδ. 21 Puech (quoted Plat., *Men*. 81B) ? As for Orphic speculation alluded to at the Theban Kabirion, see below.

Nevertheless, a particular aspect of the more familiar Dionysos, his Underworld function, could be the basis of the Mystery nature of this god, bound to disappearance and cyclic re-appearance. This Underworld element in Dionysos—as e.g. in the mythical-ritual complex of the Dionysos of Lerna—may be the reason for his involvement in the Eleusian Mysteries. On the other hand, Dionysos of the Underworld, Lord of life and death and of the boundary which separates these, would, even apart from the myth of the child Dionysos Zagreus devoured by the Titans, have been very fittingly associated with that destiny beyond death to which the soul is committed in the mysteric, as well as in the mysteriosophic vision. [4]

Iconography and history of the Mysteries of Eleusis (nos. 1-52)

Judging from iconographical testimonies the association of Dionysos with the two goddesses might date from the IVth century B.C. One of the richest and most important sources of Eleusinian theology, of shortly after the middle of the IVth century B.C., is the famous *pelike* (wine jar) in the Hermitage Museum (nos. 1 and 2). The two scenes distributed on the side of the vase seem related to each other, so that they form two coherent groups.

In the first scene Persephone, crowned with ivy, rises from the ground and offers to Hermes a white-haired child, also crowned, wrapped in a fawn skin, more probably a young Iacchus than a Plutos. Athena appears among other figures, to signify the Athenian presence at Eleusis. In the second scene are Demeter, Persephone, the child Plutos, with a cornucopia, and other figures among whom are Dionysos [5] and Herakles, in the guise of an initiate, while a female figure seated on a rock or on an *omphalos* resembles the type of Ge, the Earth. Dating from seventy years earlier is an Attic red-figured vase from Rhodes (no. 3) which shows Ge herself, emerging from the earth and offering the child Plutos, on a cornucopia, to Demeter. This reminds us of well known literary texts, such as *Od.* 5, 125 and Hesiod's *Theog.* 969. Dionysos is absent. On the other hand the myth of Iasion, father of Plutos, is explicitly referred to in a fragment of a calyx-krater in the Hermitage (3rd quarter of Vth century B.C., not shown here). A fragment of an amphora from Locri (no. 12), still more ancient (middle of VIth century B.C.) presents, among the gods of Eleusis and Athens, but without Dionysos, the figure of a bearded man with a sceptre called Ploutodotas, the 'giver of wealth', who can only be Pluton (cf. also the Paris amphora, no. 13, and the London hydria, no. 14, where the same god, Pluton, is identified not only by his horn of plenty but also by his white hair, in this resembling the child Plutos, already mentioned). This Pluton reappears, in Eleusinian ceramics, also in the scene of the Rape of Persephone and in a large fragmentary *skyphos* (deep cup) in the Eleusis Museum (c. 430 B.C.: no. 10) and in a fragment of roof ornamentation, also incomplete, in the same museum (no. 9). The return of the goddess called Pherophatta (Persephone) is represented in a krater in Dresden (no. 11) where Persephone is welcomed by Hermes, who also appeared

---

[4] Dionysos Zagreus, a boy, was torn to pieces by the Titans. Zeus struck the Titans with his thunderbolts and from their ashes and vapour were born man and (in the Neoplatonic but perhaps already Orphic interpretation: see Plat. *Leg.* 701C) the ontological evil which is revealed in man's earthly and phenomenal existence.

[5] This is true also of the Sandford-Graham pelike (no. 4). In the Capuan hydria (no. 6) Dionysos has a thyrsus of the same shape. In the Cretan hydria (no. 7) he is in the same position as in the pelike of the Hermitage.

in the scene of the Rape, and by three followers of Pan. It is clear that we are in a world of a religiosity of agrarian and cereal connotations, and this is proved by an Athenian jar (no. 15) which shows Demeter with a plough by the side of Pluton with his horn of plenty. It is unnecessary to remind the reader of the story of Triptolemos being sent round the world, a story very frequently found on the most ancient ceramics which illustrate Eleusinian subjects. The possible connection between the Eleusinian goddess and the Phrygian goddess of the earth—whose animals are the lions—is however alluded to in an Attic wine jug of the Naples Museum on which Demeter and Persephone, bearing sheaves of corn, are flanked by a lion (no. 19, but see commentary). Possible connections between Eleusis and the *Dioscuri*, gods who had much to do with initiatory rites, may be proved by an interesting wine jar in the Naples Museum (no. 39), by the Pourtales krater (no. 33) and by other sources. Finally, the two goddesses are associated with Asklepios in the context of the Epidauria Festival at Athens, on which occasion these three deities were shown together.

The introduction of Dionysos into the Eleusinian cycle in the IV century B.C. may be referred to in the fragment of a krater in the Ashmolean Museum (no. 8) on which the child on Demeter's lap, covered with a fawn skin, is supposed to be Dionysos and not Iacchus. This might lead us to presume that the child on the above mentioned jar in the Hermitage is not Iacchus but Dionysos, substituted for Plutos, who instead appears on the Rhodes *hydria* (no. 3) and perhaps in the so-called 'holy family', with Demeter and Persephone, of an Este relief in Vienna (no. 28).

Particular importance, not only in the field of iconography but also for the history of the Eleusinian cult, is attached to a Cretan *hydria* in the Athens Museum, with a scene very similar to that on a water jar from Capua, now in the Lyons Museum (no. 6), showing the two goddesses: Demeter is seated on a wicker hamper and Dionysos is seated, with his thyrsus, on an *omphalos*. According to Metzger, even the attitude of Demeter seated on the hamper is characteristic of the IVth century B.C. and is derived from a statuary group representing the mother seated and her daughter standing, although a Praxitelian group, Demeter-Persephone-Iacchus, from a temple near the Dipylon (Paus. 1,2,4) is also well known. Similar marbles, that is, with the two goddesses but also, as nos. 21 and 17, with other figures, are cited: a curly-haired Dionysos seems to stand side by side with the two goddesses (no. 17). Dionysos also appears, with other deities, in other records of the greatest interest, such as the bas-relief of Mondragone (no. 25), the sarcophagus of Torrenova (no. 47), containing a scene of an initiation ceremony, and the Lovatelli urn (no. 50) with a similar scene. It is true that these last could hardly be taken as genuine documents of the Eleusinian Mystery religion.

The Kabirian Mysteries of Thebes (nos. 53-67)

The question of the presence of Dionysos in the Demetrian Mysteries, and also of the presence of Demeter (or at least of a great chthonic goddess and mother) in the rites and myths of Dionysos, reoccurs in connection with the worship of the 'great gods' or Kabiri (the perfect equivalence of these two terms has recently been contested). Typical is the situation of the Kabirian shrine in Boeotia, near Thebes, a shrine which was the seat of the 'Mysteries', already known from literary sources and discovered by German archaeologists in 1887-88. The ἱερὸς λόγος of the Kabirion of Thebes is mentioned by Pausanias, 9, 25.

Coming from Thebes, he says, one arrives first at the little wood sacred to Demeter Kabi-
raia and Persephone, which the initiates only may enter. The shrine of the Kabiri is seven
stadia further on. He apologises for not saying what the Kabiri are or what are the *dromena*
(ritual actions) celebrated for them and for the 'Mother'; the phrase alludes to the Mystery
character of these gods. It may be that their name was never to be uttered, or that it was
covered with the seal of secrecy (a similar case to that, in Eleusis, of the so-called 'god' and
'goddess' represented in the famous relief of Lakrateides (no. 23)). But Pausanias does not
refuse to tell us what the Thebans say about the origin of these celebrations. He says there
was originally in this place a city, whose inhabitants were called Kabiri. Demeter came here
and entrusted to one of the Kabiri, Prometheus, and to his son Aitneus, a 'deposit'.
Pausanias refuses to say what this 'deposit' was and what became of it. Thus the *teleté*, the
Mystery rites, are, he tells us, a gift from Demeter to the Kabiri. There follows a series of
events in which appears the figure of a woman, Pelarge, who with her husband Isthmiades
re-established the Mysteries, suspended at the time of the expulsion of the Kabiri by
the Argians who transported them to a place called Alexiaros (the form of this name is
reminiscent of the mysterious names of the Kabiri of Samothrace). When the Mysteries
were re-established the surviving Kabiri returned to the Kabeiraia. There follow a series
of episodes intended to show the tragic end of all who violate the shrine.

It has been thought that Demeter was worshipped in the little wood near the shrine and
that it was to her alone that the women offered their gifts—for there are no traces of feminine ritual offerings on the site of the Kabirian temple, where only male worshippers offered
gifts. Certain archaeological remains like the base of a religious statue and fragments of
vases and votive objects, chief of which is the fragment (no. 53) which shows Kabiros, in
the guise of Dionysos, reclining, holding a drinking cup, and Pais, a boy cup-bearer serving
him from a krater; that central figure, called Kabiros in that fragment, Kern identifies
with the Prometheus mentioned by Pausanias. He is accompanied by his son (?) Pais who,
according to a description, still unedited, of the votive objects representing him, was even
more popular than his father with the donors.

That ceramic fragment we have just mentioned, showing Kabiros and Pais, is of great
interest for another reason too. At one end of the fragment (no. 53) is a rough caricature of
an uncouth personage, whom an inscription names as Mitos, and another of his female
companion, whom an inscription names as Krateia. To the right of these, in an attitude of
familiar cordiality, the figure, also roughly caricatured, of a personage called Pratolaos.
The name Mitos, literally the 'thread', takes us unexpectedly back to Orphic mythology
and its poetic-cosmological terminology in which, according to a saying of Epigenes recorded
by Clement of Alexandria, *mitos* signified sperm (*Strom.* V, 49 II, p.360, 10 Staehl.). So the
two characters are revealed as progenitors of the first man, here indicated as Pratolaos.
Krateia, from κράτος, indicates the concept of the generative force. This is a characteristic-
ally Orphic theme since, as is well known, the poetry inspired by Orpheus deals with speculation of a mythological, theogonical and cosmological nature, great use being made of
sexual themes (this would have been usual, later, with gnostic literature as well). Nevertheless, sexual themes, sometimes of a more crude, phallic nature, are typical of the Boeotian
ceramics found in the Theban Kabirion, where the exoteric cult certainly included agricul-
tural festivals to promote the earth's fecundity. Moreover, themes which were connected
with the 'first men' and 'primitive men' were clearly linked to the Kabirian mythological

world of Samothrace and Lemnos. This is well brought out by Kern who observes that the presence of Orphic elements in a vase of Attic origin like that in question must not surprise us. A possible hypothesis, in his opinion, is that the traces of an Orphic influence in the Theban Kabirion may have some connection with the activity of that Athenian, Methapos, who, according to Pausanias (4, 1, 7), instituted the Kabirian Mysteries of Thebes and was also active in reforming some Mystery cults. As for Kerényi's mystic interpretation of figures of birds, of various types, and for initiatory scenes, or the presence of Demeter, on the vases, see resp. no. 57 and nos. 55a and b. What is certain is that the Dionysiac and rural atmosphere of the cult is shown in the symbolic offerings (and certainly in the real offerings too) of animals, particularly bulls.

Funeral terracottas of Boeotia (no. 67, cf. no. 68)

Another group of archaeological monuments attests the presence of soteriological concepts relating to burial rites and to afterlife in the context of a Dionysiac religiosity of an Orphic type. There is a series of protomes (busts) in terracotta, found in Boeotia and the country of Locris, dating from the Vth to the IVth century B.C. In these Dionysos (or the dead?) is represented with his usual attribute of the drinking cup and with the less customary attribute of the egg. Certainly this does not in itself express the well known Orphic concept according to which the egg represents a primordial cosmogonic entity (when the cosmic egg was broken heaven and earth came out of it, and the figure of the resplendent demiurge and cosmic God Phanes). The egg motif here refers rather to funeral symbology and is a sign of life, of immortality or even of re-birth. In this respect it resembles another symbol, frequently found in these busts, the cock, which appears on some of these objects which show female figures, sometimes together with the egg symbol. Other symbols, certainly referring to the concept of a life beyond the grave, are in this same category of objects: the dove, a creature representing a great motherly deity, and the pig, the connection of which with the Demetrian and chthonic cycle is well known.

Chthonic-Mystic Religiosity in Magna Graecia

a) *The Apulian Vases* (nos. 69-77)

The terracotta protomes we have just mentioned, taken together with the Theban Kabirion, prove that there was an important centre of funeral-soteriological religiosity of a Dionysiac or even Demetriac type, but with Orphic elements, in central Greece and especially in the Boeotian region. But it is known that, apart from Athens, there was another region in which are found beliefs of a Dionysiac and Orphic nature about life after death, closely linked with the divine figures of Demeter and Persephone. This was Southern Italy, whence came the well known 'Orphic' tablets, documents in which the above-mentioned religious elements are all present—in fact, so much so that one has even suspected they belonged to the Eleusinian world of initiation Mysteries—. Later on we shall say something about the content and ideological implications of these important epigraphical documents. Here we must merely point out that ceramics and other plastic objects found in Southern Italy offer an interesting and typical *pendant* to the tablets, although in saying this we do not mean to assert that they express exactly the same type of religiosity and belief. We are referring to the tablets of Locri and the painted vases of Apulia.

As far as these are concerned, we have the most elaborate scenes on the famous vases of Altamura, Canosa and Ruvo (nos. 71, 69, 70), in which the centre of the scene more often represents the gods of the Underworld, Hades and Persephone, surrounded by a group of figures alluding to scenes of the world beyond: Orpheus (as a mystagogue? see no. 69), the sufferings of the damned, in which figures of *Dike* (Judgment: nos. 71 and 69) or of the Erinyes (nos. 69, 71, and 73) are present and participate. These personages are at home in this context and clearly associated with an eschatology of compensation, certainly akin to Orphic ways of thinking.

Other various Apulian vases represent the dead man in his *heroon*, and in these scenes the initiates' bands or fillets, *taeniae*, are very common, as in the Theban Kabirian vases, with other initiatic (or at least funeral) furniture (ball, box, basket, mirror, lyre, lynx: see nos. 74-77, with Commentary).

b) *The pinakes (votive tablets) of Locri* (nos. 60-66)

An equally obvious funerary character is seen in the Locri tablets, most of which came from a shrine of Persephone, where they had been placed as votive offerings. These votive tablets are Ionian art, many of an archaic style, and date from the period between the end of the VIth century B.C. and the years 470-460. The most frequent theme is the cult of the dead, considered as 'heroes', in the contexts of beliefs similar to those implied in the above-mentioned Apulian vases. Here also recur certain symbols, such as the box or small chest, the basket and, of special reference to the world of Beyond, the cock (see nos. 62, 64, 66).

Sometimes an allusion to death occurs in scenes of the ravishing or driving away into Hades of young women (in the first case, as. e.g. in no. 60, the dead woman holds the mystic cock; in another fragment she holds an apple). Sometimes (no. 61) the young woman who is driven (not snatch) away has an expression not of grief but of serenity, which might be explained by the prospects of life in the other world taught by an initiatory religion. In the same sample, the impassive expression of the dead woman contrasts with the attitude of the survivors who are present at her departure. It is true that a serene attitude towards death is seen on other Greek funeral monuments, beginning with the famous Attic grave stones, which have no special connection with initiatory religion. Moreover, in many of these monuments it is the disappearance of Persephone, borne away by the god of the Underworld, rather than the departure of a dead woman, that is represented. We notice, by the way, that it is always a dead woman, not a dead man. This may however be explained by the fact that the tablets were placed in a shrine of the goddess. One of the *pinakes* (no. 62) is of particular interest: it shows a 'sacred conversation' scene, with Hades, Persephone and Dionysos. Hades holds in his left hand an apple, or possibly a pomegranate, and Persephone holds a cock, while Dionysos has a drinking cup. An ornamental design of bunches of grapes confirms the significance of the presence of Dionysos, which does not seem fortuitous in this type of monument. At other times (no. 63) the god who is standing before the two Sovereigns of the Underworld is Hermes, and then it is Hades who holds a drinking cup. The heavy door of the Nether World is to be seen behind the couple.

The Dionysiac Mysteries (nos. 78-82, 83-92)

Now we turn to what are commonly known as the Dionysiac Mysteries but which—when we refer to a very specific type of documentation, belonging to the Hellenistic-Roman Age —by no means exhaust the possibilities of the links between Dionysos and the religiosity of the Mysteries. These links, as we have seen, derive from a vast series of records relating to Mysteries, from Eleusis to the Theban Kabirion, the Mysteries of Samothrace and finally the monuments attesting the 'other world' religion of the Greek cities of Southern Italy,— nothing to say about those Anatolian, Thracian-Phrygian and Cretan cults which always come up for discussion whenever we speak of problems connected with the history of Dionysos and the Greek Mysteries.

If we consider the fact that Mystery cults were held in the very secrecy of *telesteria* (initiatory shrines), and that this is an essential element in their typology, we must then admit, with M. P. Nilsson, that the cult of Dionysos, as celebrated in the trieteric rites of an orgiastic nature, described in a lively manner in the *Bacchae* of Euripides, was not properly a Mystery cult. The frenzied fury of the Maenads, of whom we know barely more than their mythological transfiguration and, more often, their partly mythological transfiguration which included certain realistic elements, expressed itself in exhausting courses across the mountains, by the light of many torches. Nor does it appear that participation in these rites was an exclusive privilege, except in so far as this privilege was inherent in the very nature of the rite, typically feminine and emotional.

We understand from Plutarch, who was familiar with Clea, the directness of the Delphic Thyiades (Bacchantes), that particular traditions concerning the meaning of the myths and the nature of the relevant deities, in particular of Dionysos, were handed down within these groups. Anyway, it is only in the Hellenistic Age that the Dionysiac cultic groups, the *thiasoi*, seem to conform more closely to the type of initiatory groups, with meetings of an esoteric type, rites of initiation, degrees and hierarchies. All this was at times accompanied by a notable degeneration of the quality of the orgiastic frenzy—as is seen in the record of the Roman scandal which provoked the special Decree of the Senate *de Bacchanalibus* of 186 B.C. On the other hand, a kind of ritualisation tended to attenuate and to channel into symbolic forms the crudest manifestations of the archaic Dionysiac 'savagery'.

Whether all this came about with a real and actual break in the continuity of the traditions, or with modifications introduced for special occasions (but which came to stay), it is nevertheless true to say that in the Hellenistic and Hellenistic-Roman period the ancient *thiasoi* of the Maenads became groups and societies (Delphic and Athenian *thyiades*; *Iobacchoi*) with clearly defined forms of association, hierarchies, sacred books and texts, and their own traditions—membership being open not only to women but also to men and boys. All this gives them the character of organised sects with their own peculiar aims and doctrines. These new *thiasoi* are therefore as different from the archaic festivities of the Maenads as from the degenerate Bacchanals of the type forbidden by the Roman Senate.

However, even these distinctions do not suffice to explain the peculiar character of the Dionysiac Mysteries in later times. In fact, if on the one hand they seem to inherit, in the new, organised, ritualised and hierarchised form, archaic elements of the Dionysiac cult (ritual inebriation and *omophagia*, the latter probably reduced to a symbolical use of flesh) on the other hand they seem to be associated with soteriological intentions which were more characteristic of the funerary cults connected with Demeter, Orpheus and Dionysos, which we have seen already existing in Magna Graecia in the Classical Age.

Fortunately it is possible to distinguish, in the general complex of archaeological records which refer to the circumstances surrounding the 'Dionysiac Mysteries' we are now discussing, one element which occurs in them all and which is peculiar to them, the wicker basket (*liknon*) containing the phallus, obviously a fertility emblem, and of the Dionysiac priapic type of fertility. Although this—from a formal point of view—links these rites and monuments to the category of the ancient fertility rites (cf. the Attic phallic rites connected with Dionysos), those same rites with which the Theban Kabirion is associated as well, the Dionysiac Hellenistic rites in question undergone an obviously mystic-soteriological transference, to the category of those rites and beliefs which we have described as mysteriosophic. In these the old *paraphernalia* are overladen with symbolic references and in fact with mystical or 'spiritual' references to happiness beyond the grave. It would seem that this transition from one ideological sphere to another took place with remarkable facility and naturalness, that is, without those signs of violent interruption we see instead in the Orphic adaptation of Dionysiac mythology. [6] I refer, for example, to the fact that the slaying of the child Dionysos-Zagreus, which probably alludes to an ancient initiatory rite of Dionysiac origin, becomes in the Orphic interpretation a horrible crime of homicide and cannibalism perpetrated on a divine victim, the occasion for the appearance of a human race which mirrored in its own nature the homicidal 'Titanic' character of the violent aggressors of Zagreus while at the same time it also stressed the boy's divine nature (see above).

Nothing of all this is apparent in the Dionysiac representations which concentrate on the motif of the *liknon* with the phallus, representations which frequently include the *genre* scene, an idyllic countryside, quite in keeping with the remote but still perceptible agrarian origin of the rite. But it must be added that a scene with the *liknon* and another with the rustic shrine looking like a shrine to Priapus (nos. 94 and 95) appear in the so-called Pythagorean basilica of Porta Maggiore, where the inspiration seems mainly Apolline (no. 93). Now this presence of the mystic phallus in contexts which may be 'Pythagorean', or at any rate faithful to the notion properly 'mysteriosophic' of imprisonement and *kolasis* (chastisement) of the spiritual and divine element in the world of matter, sexuality and generation partly explains how it is that in some aspects of Ophitic gnosticism, characterised equally by the concept of the *kolasis* of the male and divine-'pneumatic' ('spiritual') element in the feminine world of matter and of begetting, the ultimate root of the All or universal Principle could be named Priapos, the phallic and fertile deity *par excellence*. (We meet this name in Justin the Gnostic, as quoted by Hippolyt, *Refutatio*. V, 26). Here perhaps is the key to the interpretation of the great painting in the *Villa dei Misteri* at Pompei, which may indeed possibly refer to a re-interpretation of a religiosity of the Dionysiac-Priapic type, by the standards of the mysteriosophic concepts of *kolasis* and liberation of the soul, the divine element. Those Pompeian scenes were now probably intended to represent the great adventure of the soul, in the context of a nuptial symbology (above all, showing the adornment of the bride) which we have already seen present in the Apulian funeral urns.

---

[6] The only exceptions seem to be the figure of 'Aidos' fleeing from the revelation of the *liknon* (no. 88) and the figure of Erinys wielding a whip in the scene of the *kolasis* (chastisement) in the Villa dei Misteri (no. 92) which, however one may interpret it, is materially near to the scene of the *liknon*.

The soul, this divine (or perhaps merely assimilated to the divine)[7] bride of the authentic divine element, thus becomes the protagonist of the 'cycle' and passes through all those purifications and initiations referred to not only in the rich symbolism (water fowl, cocks, initiation bands or fillets, spheres, eggs, crowns, vine branches, mirrors, boxes for cosmetics, *genii* and Cupids) of the Apulian urns (and Locrian terracottas)[8] but also in that of the *Villa dei Misteri* and of other Pompeian monuments. To be sure, in the Apulian vases and Locrian terracottas the role of Persephone is accentuated, and in the Pompeian monuments the role of Dionysos, but both elements may be present (see Dionysos, or the basket with the child, in the Locrian tablets (nos. 62 and 65)).

The 'great gods' of Samothrace (nos. 58, 59) *a pressing problem which awaits solution*

Having come to the end of this Introduction, the reader may be surprised to find so little space dedicated to the Mysteries of Samothrace and of the 'great gods', although these were very popular, especially in the Hellenistic-Roman Age. This omission is due to various circumstances. Apart from the restricted space at our disposal (an excuse which after all would have been applicable to other Mystery cults and which has not prevented us from describing the Theban Kabirion and its gods) the following considerations are valid.

In spite of the great interest, for purposes of historical-religious research, of the gods of Samothrace and of all one can surmise of their mysterious mythology and ritual, which impressed even the Greeks so much because of its peculiar character, we can acquire from iconographical sources very little knowledge about these which is not conventional and entirely exoteric. But the situation is perhaps changing. The Eleusinian soil has, it would appear, already yielded all its treasures, but the Samothracian excavations, beginning with those concerned with burial grounds, seem to promise many new discoveries, at least as many as those of the Theban Kabirion. We await these with great interest.

---

[7] As in the Apuleian fable of Amor and Psyche.
[8] Cf. nos. 62, 64, 66 and nos. 74-79.

LEGENDS TO THE ILLUSTRATIONS*

1, 2. Pelike from Pavlovskoi Kurgan, near Kertsch, Pantikapaion. Leningrad, Hermitage St. 1792. Height 0.38 m. Red figures on black ground, with some parts gilded and painted in various colours; typical Kertsch example, from a rich woman's tomb. 340-330 B.C. L. Stephani: *Compte-rendu de la comm. arch.* for the year 1859, plates 1, 2; E. Gerhard: *Über den Bilderkreis von Eleusis*, Ist treatise (from the *Abhand. Königl. Akad. Wissensch. zu Berlin* 1862), Berlin 1863, plates I, II; Stephani: *Die Vasensammlung der Kaiserlichen Ermitage*, Ist part, St. Petersburg 1869, p. 320-324 ad no. 1792; A. Furtwängler-K. Reichhold: *Griechische Vasenmalerei*, series II, plates, Munich 1909, plate 70 (Text pp. 51-61); O. Waldhauer: *Die Vasensammlung der Kaiserlichen Ermitage*, St. Petersburg (1906), plates II, III; P. Ducati: *Nota su alcuni monumenti relativi a divinità di Eleusi, Rendiconti Accad. Lincei*, Series V, vol. XVII, 1909, pp. 375-390; H. Metzger: *Les représentations dans la céramique attique du IVe siècle*, Bibliothèque des Écoles Françaises d'Athènes et de Rome, 172, Paris 1951, plate VIII, 3 and pp. 103 and 244; Erika Simon: *Neue Deutung zweier eleusinischen Denkmäler des IV Jahd. v. Chr.*, in *Antike Kunst* 9, 1966, pp. 72-82 (bibl.) (critical commentary by H. Metzger: *Revue des Études Grecques* 81, 1968, p. 159 et seq.); H. Metzger *Recherches sur l'imagerie athénienne*, Paris 1965, p. 40, no. 35 and plate XXIV.

There is some doubt as to whether the figures on the two sides, A and B (= 1 and 2), are objectively connected, and whether B (= 2) represents a 'dynamic' composition, that is, a scene of action. Simon thinks it does, but is opposed by Furtwängler, because of the statuesque pose of certain figures.

A (= 1): in the centre is Demeter with sceptre and *polos* (headgear) or crown (similar to the figure of Hera on side B (=2)), seated on a rock (Simon); on her right is a youth with two torches, in the attitude of a mystagogue or a *daduchos* (torchbearer). He has long curly hair, a crown of leaves, a long-sleeved tunic and leggings. According to Furtwängler this figure represents Eumolpos and is similar to figures on the Pourtalès vase (no. 33) and on the Niinnion tablet (see also the inscription [Eumol]pos on a torchbearer of a hydria in Boston: Nicole, *Meidias*, Plate V, 1). Other interpretations: Iacchos (see nos. 3 and 4), Eubuleus. In front are Demeter and Triptolemos on his winged chariot. To the left of the goddess is the young Plutos, with diadem and cornucopia, and behind him is Kore, with a torch. In the two top corners are Herakles, to the left, crowned with myrtle, holding his club in his right hand and the bakchos, the initiate's bunch of leaved branches, in his left, and to the right is Dionysos crowned with ivy and with a thyrsus in his hand. Below, to the left, is Aphrodite with a small winged Eros. To the far right is the matronly figure of a goddess seated on a round stone, an *omphalos* (Ducati), which has a sort of base. On the *omphalos* is a cloth; she looks at Demeter and Kore. The matronly figure, used to represent several goddesses, here probably stands for Gaia or Themis (according to Simon: Rhea).

* Thanks are due to Professor Paolino Mingazzini who kindly read the manuscript and gave useful suggestions.

B (=2): a new born baby is wrapped in a *nebris*, a fawn skin (according to Simon he is Zagreus, according to Furtwängler, Iacchos and according to Metzger Dionysos). He is presented to Hermes by a female who rises from the ground (Simon: Persephone; Metzger: Dirce). Cf. below the hydria from Rhodes. Both the female figure and the child appear to be crowned with ivy. The central figure is Athena, of a statuesque type (Furtwängler) whose presence may be explained by the Athenian interest in Eleusis; to the left a young female figure seated on a sort of pedestal, different in shape from the *omphalos*, is beating a kettledrum. Above, from the right, are Hera, Zeus, a Nike, a goddess with two torches and a young girl.

3. Hydria from Rhodes. Museum of Istanboul. Height 0.46 m. Attic vase with three handles, red figures of the same style and same period as the Kertsch pelike; from a tomb; IVth century B.C. S. Reinach: *La naissance de Ploutos sur un vase découvert à Rhodes, Revue Archéologique*, 3rd Series, vol. 36, 1900, pp. 87-98, fig. on p. 93; Furtwängler-Reichhold: *Griech. Vasenmalerei*, cit., Series II, Text p. 59, fig. 25; Metzger; *Représentations*, cit. p. 244 et seq. (bibl.) and Plate XXXII.—Gaia offers, on a cornucopia, he child Plutos (or Brimos?; Furtwängler: the child Iacchus) to Demeter (?) his mother—Hes: *Theog.* 969, cp. *Od.* V, 125 and Aristoph.: *Thesmoph.* 295; Athen.: *Deipnosoph.* 15, 30, concerning the birth of Plutos from Demeter. (According to Mingazzini: Plutos and Eirene). According to Kieseritzky the fragment of an Attic krater in the Hermitage (1889, 1) dating from the 3rd quarter of the Vth century, with the inscription ΙΑΣΣΟΣ alludes to the tragic end of the loves of Demeter and Iasion; cf. Metzger: *Recherches* cit. p. 7 et seqt., no. 1 and Plate I). Behind the standing goddess is Iacchus, with a rich tunic, high leggings, a crown and two torches. A female figure, Persephone if the former figure is Demeter, bears two torches; at the two top corners are Aphrodite and a male figure (Hermes?) which reminds us of figures in a similar attitude on the Apulian vases. It is impossible to identify the other two female figures. In the centre, above, is Triptolemos.

4. Pelike from the former Sandford-Graham Collection, from Athens. Reproduction from the frontispiece of the Sales Catalogue of this Collection in Metzger: *Recherches* cit., p. 34, no. 2, Plate XIV, I.—In the centre Demeter is seated on a magnificent woven basket; she is crowned with ears of corn and bears a sceptre. In front of her is the child Plutos with the cornucopia. To the left are Persephone (Kore) with two torches and Hermes (Metzger), to the right Dionysos with a long *chiton* and *himation*, holding a thyrsus, and also Iacchus, a figure similar to Nos. 1 and 3 and the Niinnion tablet.

5. Hydria (water jar) with decoration in relief, from Cumae. Hermitage 51659, height 0.655 m. IVth century B.C. Stephani: *Vasensammlung* cit. no. 525; Gerhard: *Eleus. Bilderkreis*, cit., Plate 3 (drawing); Overbeck: *Kunstmythologie*, III, p. 510 and chap. XI. Atlas Plate XVIII, no. 20; Gabrici: *Monumenti ant. dei Lincei* 22, 1914, Plates 101, 102; Ducati: *Rendiconti Lincei*, 1909, cit.; Metzger: *Recherches* cit. p. 40, no. 36 and Plates XX, XXI, XXII. Frieze, with gilding, around the neck of the vase.—In the centre Demeter seated on a hamper (?) with sceptre and *kalathos* (basket) is turning towards Kore who has a torch; between them are two *bakchoi* crossed over a *plemochoe* (a kind of vessel used in Eleusine ritual to pour a libation in the last day of the celebration) from which some stalks (Metzger)

or flames arise. The fact that the lid, with its relief decoration, is missing makes the form of the vase different from that of the *kernos* (*kerchnos*) of which the little flames or stalks remind us (cf. *kerchnos* of nos. 35 and 41). To the left are Dionysos with his thyrsus and long tunic, Triptolemos with his winged chariot and serpents, a male figure with boots and a great torch, and a goddess who somewhat resembles Demeter (or Rhea?) seated on an altar (or an *omphalos* with drapery and base?). To the right is Herakles holding a little pig, a club and a bunch, Athena, a young male figure of the Iacchus type (cf. the preceding nos.), according to Stephani an Eubuleus with two torches, and finally a seated female figure sceptred, different from the figure exactly opposite (Aphrodite?). The trivet on the little column behind Dionysos is characteristic.

6.   Hydria from Capua, from the former Tyszkiewicz Collection. Lyons Museum. Height 0. 465 m. IVth century B.C. W. Fröhner: *La Collection Tyszkiewicz*, Munich (1892) Plates IX and X; G. Barracco: *Notizie degli Scavi*, 1883, p. 49; *Monumenti dell' Instituto* XII, Plate 34; Metzger: *Représentations* cit., p. 243, no. 10, Plate 28, I; id. *Recherches*, cit., p. 37 no. 18 and Plate XVII. Large hydria with polychrome decoration and gilding (white figures, the two goddesses, and red on black) with three handles, from S. Maria di Capua Vetere. —Two crossed ears of corn, belonging to a garland, surmount the central figure. Persephone, crowned with laurel, has two torches; she stands between Demeter, crowned, with a sceptre tipped with lilies, who is seated on a throne with characteristic horizontal bands (a hamper?) and Dionysos, robed and bearing a thyrsus with knotted serpents, seated on an *omphalos* (Rubensohn: *Athen. Mitteil.* 24, p. 56: Iacchus [?]). To the left the 'king of Eleusis' (Metzger) and at the sides two Maenads, one of whom has a kettledrum. There is no reason to believe that the scene is set in the Underworld.

7.   Hydria from Crete. National Museum, Athens, 1443. IVth century B.C. Metzger: *Recherches* p. 39, no. 31. Plate XIX, I; Mylonas: Ἐφημερὶς Ἀρχαιολογική 1960, p. 105, fig. 143; Metzger: *Représentations* p. 243, no. 9, Plate 34, 3.—Similar to the preceding figure, with its crossed ears of corn and representation of divine figures. Demeter's throne '*à double degré*'. Behind Demeter a personage of the Iacchus type (see above). Two other figures.

8.   Fragment of a bell krater from Al-Mina. Oxford, Ashmolean Museum 1956-355. Metzger: *Recherches* p. 52 et seq., cf. p. 38 no. 21, Plate XXV, 2. IVth century B.C.—Persephone standing, to the left, with two torches; Demeter seated on a throne, holds on her lap a little boy dressed in a short sleeved chiton, a fawn skin and boots (Dionysos); two other figures at the sides (Metzger: Hermes and Ares? but perhaps more probably Athena?). The figure of Dionysos is of a singular type; Metzger attributes this to the Eleusinian influence (Demeter as a mother; for Demeter holding an adult Persephone on her knees, see below, no. 22).

9.   Fragments of a tympanum from a sacred Eleusinian building, Eleusis Museum. Maximilian Mayer: Ἐφημ. Ἀρχαιολ., 1893, coll. 191-200, Plate XIV.—Rape of Persephone. The figures of Pluto, Persephone, Eros and the chariot itself are missing. There remain, from the right, the figures of Artemis, present height c. 0.50 m (original height c. 0.80 m.), Athena, Hermes and, most probably, Hecate.

10. Fragmentary *skyphos* from the Eleusinian shrine. Eleusis Museum, 1244. Total height c. 0.25 m, c. 430 B.C. P. Hartwig: *Der Raub der Kora auf einem Vasenbilde in Eleusis, Athenische Mitteilungen* 21, 1896, p. 377 et seqq., 384, Plate 12; Kourouniotes: *Eleusis. A Guide to the excavations and the museum*, Athens 1936, p. 116 et seq.; cf. Metzger: *Recherches*, p. 11 no. 6 (which also refers, p. 10 no. 5, to an amphora in the National Museum of Naples, 3091, Förster: *Raub und Rückkehr der Persephone*, Plate 2; these are the only two vase paintings of the Eleusinian myth of the rape of Persephone which date from the Vth century, B.C.). Vase with red figures with inscription of the dedicator (Anthippe) in the style which Furtwängler calls *streng-schön* (to be dated 480-470).—The chariot of Hades is sinking into the ground (the χάσμα γῆς). Eros flies above it, bearing a crown and a torch. Hermes seems to be making a gesture of farewell. In the background may have been Demeter, sceptred, and to the left Hecate (Metzger; according to Hartwig: Artemis) and a sea nymph. Metzger: *'reflet d'une composition grandiose, qui ne se conçoit pas en dehors de la legende du hiéron'*. The scene of the rape is instead frequently found in the Roman period, on sarcophaghi as well as on the frontal described in no. 9 and in the terracottas of Locri (see below).

11. Krater with inscriptions, Dresden Museum 350. Zug.-Verz. Nr. 926; height 0.370 m. P. Hermann: *Erwerbungen der Antikensammlungen in Deutschland: Dresden*; 1891, *Archäolog. Anzeiger* 7, 1892, p. 166 et seq. (bibl.) fig. 33; Metzger: *Recherches* p. 13, no. 15. Red figured, elegant style.—*Anodos* (return) of Persephone (inscription: Φ[Ε]ΡΟΦΑΤΤΑ), with a diadem, turning to Hermes, by whom she is welcomed, to the joy of the followers of Pan (with inscriptions difficult to interpret). At other times the goddess is welcomed by the Satyrs, but sometimes the goddess welcomed by a follower of Pan is Aphrodite (Metzger: op. cit. p. 13, no. 18). In either case it is clear that the theme is the reawakening of the fertile forces of nature. But sometimes the woman who rises from the earth is Pandora and satyrs with great hammers, or even Gaia, are present at her arrival. The return of Persephone is shown also in the bell krater of the Vasto Collection, now at the Metropolitan Museum of New York, 28.57.23: Persephone, who issues from the χάσμα is led by Hermes and Hecate to her mother, whom she greets. Hecate seems almost to 'evoke' Persephone (inscription: ΠΕΡΣΩΦ ΑΤΑ). J. Overbeck: *Atlas der Griech. Kunstmythologie*, 4 Liefer., Leipzig 1878, Plate XVIII, 15; id,. *Kunstmythol.* III p. 663; Strube: *Suppl. zu den Studien über d. Bilderkreis von Eleusis*, Plate III; Kourouniotes: Κόρης ἄνοδος in Δελτίον 15, 1933-35, p. 4, fig. 3 (photo); Metzger: *Recherches* p. 11 no. 7. On this subject see M.P. Nilsson: *Die Anodos der Pherephatta auf den Vasenbildern, Opuscula Selecta* II, p. 611 et seq.

12. Fragment of an amphora from Locri, Museum of Reggio Calabria 4001. Middle of VIth century B.C. (With some figures). Metzger: *Recherches* p. 8 et seqq. no. 2, Plates I, 2 and II, 1 and 2. Attic style, with inscriptions, and therefore to be distinguished for its regional and historical characteristics from the Locri tablets (see below nos. 60-66).—A goddess with chariot and ears of corn (not here reproduced) is presumably Demeter (rather than Persephone who was a favourite subject in local art) in the act of leaving or arriving at Eleusis. Triptolemos (with inscription), crowned with ears of corn and with ears of corn in his left hand, Athena, Herakles, Hermes (not reproduced here), then a bearded figure with a sceptre, with an inscription: Πλουτοδότας (a name of Pluton).

13.   Neck amphora, red figured, from the Louvre, G 209, Height 0.25 m. *Corpus vasorum antiquorum*, France 9 Louvre 6 III I c Plate 38, 10-11.39, 1 (Fr. 417. 418); K. Schauenburg: *Pluton und Dionysos, Jahrb. deutsch. arch. Instituts* 68, 1953, pp. 38-72 and p. 41, fig. 4; Metzger: *Recherches* p. 23 no. 57.—Pluton has a sceptre and a cornucopia, brimfull with bunches of grapes and other fruit, and something which resembles fig. no. 15. He stands before Persephone who has a phiale (flat bowl) and a wine ladle (*oinochoe*). Pluton with his wealth drawn from the mines seems to have given place her, through the influence of Eleusis, to Pluton rich in fruits. Pluton is already mentioned in I. G. I, 2, 5 from Eleusis, c. 500 B.C. but Plutos first appears in literature (Hes. *Theog.* 969 et seqq.; for a list of his representations see Zwicker: *RE* XXI, I, 1027 et seqq. under Plutos). Pluton instead first appears in figurative art; the former is probably another aspect of the latter. The two are not interchangeable from the archeological point of view (Schauenburg). Metzger: *Recherches* p. 24 et seqq. no. 60 refers to the medallion on a red figured goblet in the British Museum, E 82 (see also Nilsson: *Archiv für Religionswissensch.* 32, 1935, p. 90 *Opuscula Selecta* II, p. 556) where Pluton, crowned with laurel, and with a cornucopia and a *phiale*, is half reclining on a banqueting couch. This is really Pluton and not a 'Dionysos of the Underworld' (see *Bulletin de Corresp. Hellénique* 68-69, 1944-45, p. 318 et seq.).

14.   Hydria from the British Museum E 183, 2nd half of the Vth century, B.C. *Corpus Vasorum Antiquorum*, Great Britain 8 Brit. Mus. 6 III I c Plate 84, 2 c (Gr. Brit. 359); Schauenburg: *Jahrb.* 68, cit., p. 42 no. 8 (bibl.) and p. 48 et seqq.; Metzger: *Représentations* p. 234 et seq. The vase is hown in a drawing in Overbeck: *Atlas*, Plate XV, 31 (scenes of the departure of Triptolemos on his mission) cf. *Kunst-Mythol.*, III, p. 543, no. 48 (cf. also *Mon. dell'Inst.* I, Plate 4). Attic vase with red figures.—Hecate with torches and Pluton (or Plutos: Zwicker; Schauenburg is for Pluton, Nilsson is undecided: *Gesch. d. griech. Rel.*, I, respectively pp. 296 and 442. The old Plutos of Aristoph., *Plutos* v. 265, is for comic effect); the god is an old man with white hair (see also below, no. 16), a sceptre and brimming cornucopia. Here the god belongs to the Eleusinian cycle (Schauenburg).

15.   Pelike (wine jar) in the Nat. Museum of Athens 16346. Schauenburg: *Jahrb.* 68 cit. p. 42 no. 7, fig. 5; Metzger: *Recherches* pp. 23-26.—Pluton, a youthful figure, with a brimming cornucopia, from which poppy leaves are falling (Metzger: or drops of some liquid?) is shown as Πλουτοδότης (cf. no. 12), in front of Demeter who has a plough. Schauenburg refers to Demeter Πλουτοδότειρα (*Diodor.* 1, 12, 4) and Iacchus Πλουτοδότης of *Schol.* Aristoph. *Ranae* 479.

16.   Faliscan skyphos (deep cup) in Heidelberg. Schauenburg: *Jahrb.* 68 cit., p. 38 et seq. figs. 1 and 2 and p. 55.—Pluton with white hair, beardless, crowned and with a cornucopia. Silenus with a kettledrum. Feline animal rising from the ground, and a crane.

17.   Votive relief from Eleusis. Eleusis Museum. Two fragments of Pentelic marble height respectively 0.36 m and 0.18 m, thickness 0.11 m. O. Kern: *Athenische Mitteilungen* 17, 1892, p. 127 fig. 2 and p. 128; G.E. Rizzo: *Römische Mitteilungen* 25, 1910, p. 135, fig. 12 (*ibid.* Bielefeld, p. 7 no. 8); Metzger: *Recherches* p. 35 no. 9.—Demeter seated on a hamper (cylindrical, divided in two by a horizontal band, cf. no. 20) without a sceptre

(Metzger); Persephone with two torches, Dionysos with curled hair and a fawn skin. In the right hand fragment Pluton or θεός (the God, by analogy with the Lakrateides relief: Kern), then a lyre player and the remains of a female figure. Of rather more recent date than the Mondragone relief (no. 23): Mingazzini: *Notizie degli Scavi* 1927, p. 312.

18.   Volute-krater from tomb no. 128 of the Necropolis of Spina. Spina Museum. Height 0.56 m (0.655 with the volutes), width of mouth 0.42 m. Second half of the Vth century B.C. F. Sartori: *Rendiconti Accad. Naz. dei Lincei* 5, 1950, pp. 233-258, figs. 1 and 2; M.P. Nilsson: *Dionysiac Mysteries* pp. 24-26 (bibl.) and p. 25 fig. 3. Attic red figured vase with inscriptions.—It represents Dionysos-Bacchus and Demeter-Chloe. The goddess has a lion or lioness on her left arm, which holds a sceptre; in her right hand is a *phiale* (bowl). They are in a temple, indicated by two columns; on the ground in front is an altar (Mingazzini, verbal communication) full of firewood. A woman bears the *liknon* (wicker cradle), covered, but without the phallus. Then come women with cymbals, kettledrums and serpents. The identity of the gods is uncertain. The lion appears to be connected with the influence of the worship of the Great Mother (see *Eurip., El.* 1301 et seq. and no. 19).

19.   *Olpe* (wine jug), black figured, from the Astarita Collection Naples. Metzger: *Recherches* p. 22 et seqq. no 43 and Plate VIII.—Demeter and Persephone standing, with very long-stalked ears of corn; they are accompanied by a lion (see no. 18 and no. 14). According to Mingazzini (verbal communication) the lion seems to be a bad restoration of a dog.

20.   Votive relief from Eleusis. Eleusis Museum. Found in the vicinity of the so-called *bouleuterion*. Height 0.48 m, width 0.42 m. Kern: *Athenische Mitteilungen*, 17, 1892, p. 129 fig. 4; Studniczka: *Jahrb.* 19, 1904, p. 7, fig. 4; Bielefeld: *Wissensch. Ztschr. d. Univ. Greifswald*, Jahrg. I 1951-52. Gesellsch. und Sprachswiss. Reihe no. 2-3, p. 8 no. 24; Mylonas: *Eleusis* p. 190 fig. 63; Metzger: *Recherches* p. 35 no. 7.—Demeter seated on a hamper, cylindrical and divided in two by a horizontal band which suggests a lid (Mingazzini, see also no. 17). Persephone standing.

21.   Small marble group in the Eleusis Museum. Height 0.30 m, width 0.22 m. Kern: *Athenische Mitteilungen*, 17, 1892, p. 132, fig. 9; Metzger p. 35 no. 6.—Demeter seated on a hamper. Persephone, standing, places a hand on Demeter's shoulder. The hamper still bears traces of red colour. Near Demeter there was another figure. The group was originally on a base.

22.   Small marble group from Eleusis. Eleusis Museum. Height c. 0.30 m. IVth century B.C. D. Philios: *Athenische Mitteilungen* 20, 1895, p. 249 n. 1 and 358 et seq., fig. p. 359. Furtwängler: *Masterpieces* p. 461; Picard: *Bulletin de corresp. hellén.* 55, 1931, p. 16; Kourouniotes: *Eleusis*, p. 98, fig. 43.—Persephone is seated on her mother's knees, her left hand resting on her shoulder. This group may be modelled on a statuary group of the end of the Vth century or the first half of the IVth century, B.C.

23.   Lakrateides relief. Eleusis Museum. Most of the fragments come from the Plutonion.

Height 1.80 m, width originally c. 3 m; date c. 100-90 B.C. D. Philtios: Ἐφημερὶς Ἀρχαιολο-
γικὴ 1886, coll. 19-32 and Plate 3; R. Heberdey: *Das Weiherelief des Lakrateides aus Eleusis, Festschrift Benndorf*, Vienna 1898, pp. 111-116, plate IV; Mylonas: *Eleusis*, pp. 197-199
(bibl.) and fig. 71.—Monument set up by Lakrateides ἱερεὺς Θεοῦ καὶ Θεᾶς καὶ Εὐβουλέω[ς
καὶ....] and offered Δήμητρι καὶ Κόρη[ι καὶ Θε]ῶι καὶ Θε[ᾶι καὶ Εὐ]βουλεῖ. From the second
figure on the left: Demeter, Persephone, Triptolemos; above is Pluton, then a goddess and
a god, who is seated, identified with the 'goddess' and 'god' mentioned in the inscription
who set us a problem concerning their real identity but appear to represent a married
couple (the king and queen of Hades?) added to the mother-daughter couple (Demeter and
Persephone) generally indicated by the words: 'the two goddesses' (see no. 24). The other
figures apparently represent the dedicator and members of his household or even (in the
case of one figure) the city.

24.   Lysimachides relief from Plutonion, Eleusis. Nat. Museum, Athens. Philios: Εφημ.
Ἀρχαιολ. 1886, cit. plate 3; Farnell: *Cults of the Greek States*, III plate I; Mylonas: *Eleusis*,
p. 198.—The two couples referred to in no. 23 are seated at a banquet: the 'two goddesses'
and the 'god' and 'goddess' (this latter couple attested as such by an inscription).

25.   Bas-relief from Mondragone. Nat. Museum of Naples. Found in 1916 in a locality
usually identified with the site of the ancient Sinuessa. Height 0.70 m, width 1.33 m. thickness 0.17. 370-360 B.C. P. Mingazzini: *Notizie degli Scavi* 1927, p. 309 et seq. plate 24;
Bielefeld: *Zum Relief aus Mondragone, Wissensch. Ztschr. d. Univ. Greifswald*, 1951-52, cit.
p. 1 et seqq.; Mylonas: Ἐφημ. Ἀρχαιολ. 1960, p. 106, fig. 15. Mingazzini: apparently of Pentelic
marble, Attic style, Praxitelian period. It probably came from Eleusis where it may have
been taken as war booty. Other scholars think there may have been a centre of Eleusinian
Mysteries in this region but there are no proofs of this. Metzger: *Recherches*, p. 36, no. 14.—
From the left: group formed by Triptolemos standing before Demeter, who is seated on a
hamper. By the side of Triptolemos stands Persephone with two torches, and perhaps the
personification of Eleusis. To the right are Hermes (Mingazzini: Eubuleus), Zeus and, at
the end, Dionysos with boots and fawn skin. Mingazzini interprets the figures differently.
Rejecting the suggestion that one figure represents a female initiate, or is a personification
of Eleusis, he interprets the figure on the hamper as the 'goddess' mentioned in the relief
of Lakrateides (no. 23), and the figure next to her as Demeter (cf. no. 26); he thinks the
seated male figure is the corresponding 'god' (reference to inscriptions).

26.   Marble relief from Eleusis. Philios: *Athenische Mitteilungen* 20, 1895, p. 252 et seq
plate VI. Type of IVth century B.C. Possibly from the Plutonion.—Persephone with two
torches, Triptolemos in a chariot with winged serpents, Demeter, and four worshippers.

27.   Large relief from Eleusis. Nat. Museum of Athens, 126. A cast is in the Eleusis
Museum. Stele of Pentelic marble. Height of the female figures 1.98 m, width of stele 1.52
thickness 0.16; bas-relief. Notwithstanding 'archaic' elements, dates from 3rd quarter of
Vth century; 'Periclean age, period of Pheidias's activity'; found in 1859 on the site of the
church of St Zacharias. J.N. Svoronos: *Das Athener Nationalmuseum*, Athens 1908-12
pp. 106-120, plates XXIV, XXV; R.R. Holloway: *The date of the Eleusis relief, American*

Journal of Archeology, 62, 1958, pp. 404-408, plate 110, fig. I; Mylonas: *Eleusis*, p. 192 et seq. fig. 68.—The figures are generally interpreted, from the left, as Demeter, Triptolemos, Persephone; Svoronos: Demeter, Nisos, Persephone. The youth is, according to Welcker, Iacchus: according to Stephani, a youthful Plutos, according to others a παῖς ἀφ'ἑστίας μυηθείς (nos. 43-45), or a youthful victor in the Eleusinian games, or a noble consecrated to the worship of the two goddesses. The figure on the right must be Persephone, by analogy with the corresponding figure of the Lakrateides relief (no. 23). Originally Demeter held ears of corn in her right hand, but these are no longer visible. She seems also to be admonishing the youth before giving him an object, no longer visible, possibly a ring. Persephone's gesture also is variously interpreted: is she crowning the youth? Is she conferring on him, as a mark of privilege, a golden curl? (see Svoronos pp. 108-112).

28.   Relief from the former Este Collection in the Catajo castle (228), now in the Kunsthistorisches Museum, Vienna, 1095. Pentelic marble; Attic origin, end of Vth century B.C. with inscription added at a later date, which would suggest a re-utilisation of it in the IInd century B.C. (I.G. II/III² 4926 a.). O. Walter: *Die Heilige Familie von Eleusis, Jahreshefte des Österr. archäol. Instituts*, 30, 1936, pp. 50-70, plate I; M.P. Nilsson: *Archiv für Religionswiss.* 34, 1937, pp. 108-110, plate I, = *Opuscula Selecta* II, p. 624 et seq., fig. I; Metzger: *Recherches*, p. 38 no. 25.—Demeter seated, Persephone holding one torch aloft, with the other pointing to the ground in the direction of a seated boy (?), possibly to purify the child with fire and smoke (see similar scenes in the consecration of Herakles, nos. 47, 49). The alleged figure of the child would have been obliterated at the time of the re-utilisation of the relief. There is also a male figure: thus we would have Demeter, Persephone, the infant Plutos, and Zeus his father. Nilsson instead interprets the figures as Metanira, Demeter, Demophoon and Keleos. The infant would have been seated on the ground, or possibly in a cradle (*liknon*).

29.   Relief from the ruins of the Asklepieion, Athens. Girard: *L'Asclépieion d'Athènes* (*Bibl. Ec. Franç. d'Athènes et de Rome* 23) Paris 1881, pp. 43-49 and plate II; Foucart: *Les Mystères d'Eleusis*, p. 322.—Demeter, seated on a hamper, Persephone with two torches, Asklepios and worshippers. Asklepios in an attitude similar to that of other *ex voto* in the temple. The figures are shown within a temple. The scene represented probably refers to the Epidauria, a festival which is connected with the Eleusinian cycle. On the architrave are the names of the worshippers but below, between columns, are only five names. The people concerned are probably officials who supervised the festival and were crowned there. The letter E may mean Ἐπιδαύρια.

30.   Relief and inscription of the Rheitoi. Eleusis Museum. Maximum height 0.83 m, width 0.57 m. Stele of Pentelic marble. D. Philios: *Athenische Mitteilungen*, 19, 1894, pp. 163-193, plate VII; Mylonas: *Eleusis*, fig. 69.—Demeter, with Persephone who points one torch towards the ground, perhaps for some purificatory purpose. The personification of Eleusis greets Athena. The inscription bears the date 421 B.C. It is a decree of the people's assembly and the Council which provides for the building of a bridge to facilitate the transport, in solemn procession, of the 'sacred objects' used in the celebration of the Mysteries: ὡς ἂν τὰ ἱερὰ φέρωσιν αἱ ἱέρειαι ἀ[σ]φαλέστατα.

31. 'Praxitelian' head, possibly of Eubuleus, from Eleusis. Nat. Museum of Athens. A very famous piece, discussed by Furtwängler: *Masterpieces*, pp. 330 et seqq., plate XVI. —Identification has been the subject of dispute. The mystical expression of the face and the treatment of the head remind G. E. Rizzo (*Römische Mitteilungen* 25, 1910, p. 112 and n. 1 bibl.) of the figure of Iacchos on the Torrenova sarcophagus (no. 47). Rizzo therefore questions the identification of this fragment (head, bust) with the Praxitelian Eubuleus, which Furtwängler maintains.

32. Fragments of a pyxis found in the Eleusinian shrine. Eleusis Museum. Polychrome terracotta with figures in relief. Rubensohn: *Eleusinische Beiträge, Athenische Mitteilungen* 24, 1899, pp. 55-59, plate VIII, 2-3; Metzger: *Recherches*, p. 34, no. 4.—Demeter is seated on a hamper, the form of which resembles not so much nos. 5, 2 and 6 as that on the Cretan hydria (no. 7). By the side of the goddess is an incense burner on a tripod, whereas in the hydria of Cuma (5, 2) beside the goddess there is a *plemochoe* with initiatory bunches and other objects characteristic of the Eleusinian rites (Rubensohn). It is difficult to identify the object to the right of the incense burner and the figure to the left of Demeter (Persephone? Iacchos?). Further on to the left is a youth with an object which Rubensohn compares to the *bakchos* of the three initiates in no. 33 but which we consider more reminiscent of the 'pilgrim's staff' of the '*mystai*'(?) in the second position from the left of the upper and lower processions of the Niinnion tablet (no. 35); the same personage holds by the paw an animal, probably a sheep, clearly enough not a pig, and this distinguishes this representation from analogous types with references to Eleusis (see the Herakles of the hydria of Cuma, no. 5, 3). But Metzger thinks that the animal is either a pig or a dog. On the other hand Furtwängler: *Athen. Mitteil.* 20, 1895, p. 357 considers a representation of this type to be connected with Eubuleus, the 'Shepherd'; however he identifies as Eubuleus another figure who appears next to the presumed Eubuleus with the little pig on the hydria of Cuma already quoted. This, as Rubensohn points out, implies a contradiction.

33. Bell-Krater Pourtalès, Brit. Museum, F. 68 (A). Metzger: *Représentations* cit. p. 245 no. 13, plate 33,3; Mylonas: 'Εφημ. 'Αρχαιολ. 1960, p. 96 et seq.; Metzger: *Recherches* p. 39 no 27.—In the foreground Demeter seated on a cushion (Metzger) or on a throne covered with a cloth; Persephone and Triptolemos, with a throne adorned with winged serpents. Behind Herakles, with a club, and the Dioskuroi. All three have the *bakchos* and they are led by Iacchus and Eumolpos (or Eubuleus? Metzger). On side B group of Dionysos and Plutos with Hephaistos.

34. *Skyphos* (deep cup) from Capua, from the former Somzée Collection, Brussels Museum A 10. *Corpus Vasorum Antiquorum* 2, plate 18/1 b; Beazley: *Attic Red-figure Vase Painters*[2], p. 661, 86; Metzger: *Recherches* p. 28, no. 63, plate XIII, 2.—Hierophant with two torches, between Iolaos and Herakles, represented as initiates, with crown, apparently myrtle, and bunch. Herakles, distinguishable by his club, holds a *bakchos* and a small branch. Possibly this refers to a preliminary rite of purification (Metzger).

35. *Pinax* (votive tablet) dedicated by Niinnion. Athens, Nat. Museum 11036. Reproduction in the Eleusis Museum. Work of IVth century, B.C. An inscription by the dedicato

(possibly a hetaera) to the 'two goddesses'. Total height 0.44 m, width 0.32 m. Found in 1895 in the shrine, in the excavations of the south courtyard, near the wall, Γ-Γ', together with another votive tablet: Πρακτικὰ τῆς ἐν ᾿Αθην. ᾿Αρχαιολογικῆς ῾Εταιρίας 1895, p. 171 and fig. 1 (the second pinax shown in fig. 2). A.N. Skias: ᾿Εφημ. ᾿Αρχαιολ. 1901, coll. 1-50, plate I; Ducati: *Rendiconti Accad. Naz. Lincei* 1908, p. 375 et seqq.; Mylonas: *Eleusis*, fig. 88; Metzger: *Recherches* p. 31 et seq. no. 70; Erika Simon: *Neue Deutung zweier eleusinischer Denkmäler des 4. Jahrs. v. Chr.*, *Antike Kunst* 9, 1966, pp. 86-91; this author believes that the tablet does not refer to the Mystery rites but to the Eleusinian festival of the *Haloa*, an interpretation contested by H. Metzger: *Revue des Etudes Grecques* 81 (1968), p. 159 et seq.— The scene is arranged on two planes, inside a shrine (see column above, on the left). Two processions move from left to right, the upper one towards Demeter (Metzger thinks her seat is a low cushion) and the lower one towards a goddess on a similar seat. The upper procession is led by a woman with two torches; then comes a woman with a myrtle branch who wears on her head, tied with linen bands, a *kerchnos* adorned with little branches; then comes a boy, crowned, with a jar, a branch of myrtle and a 'pilgrim's staff' (Metzger) and an adult, also crowned, with two small branches and a stick. In the lower plane, in front of the goddesses who have sceptres and *phialai*, is an *omphalos*, with two wands in front of it. Then comes a youth, crowned, with boots and long braided hair, with two torches, of the Iacchus type; then comes a woman, crowned, with a branch and stick similar to that of the first man in the upper procession, on her head a *kerchnos* adorned with small branches; behind is a male figure, crowned, with a stick over his shoulder. White stripes along the ground make it doubtful whether the figures are following each other and therefore whether it is really a case of two processions, as Nilsson thinks (*Gesch. d. griech. Relig.*, I², p. 444); he believes that the upper procession is led by Persephone, in that period of the year in which she is in Eleusis, and the lower procession by Iacchus, in that period when Persephone is absent. The *phiale* attribute suggests that the goddess in the lower procession is Kore herself in the guise of Persephone, which better corresponds to the text of the dedicatory inscription. As regards the eventual demonstrative value of the tablet for the purposes of the Mystery ceremonies, one must remember that it was set up inside the sanctuary.

36.   Red figured *stamnos*, in the Eleusis Museum, 636; side A. From a tomb in Eleusis which possibly belonged to an initiate: Kourouniotes, p. 223. Kourouniotes: ᾿Ελευσινιακὴ δᾳδουχία, ᾿Εφημ. ᾿Αρχαιολ. 1937, pp. 227-230, figg 1-4 and 9-10; Mylonas: *Eleusis* p. 209 and fig. 78; Beazley: *Attic red-figure vase-painters* ², p. 1052, 23; Metzger: *Recherches* p. 29, no. 58.—The procession is led by the *daduchos* (torch-bearer), with two torches; he is crowned with myrtle and has a mitre; he wears a typical short tunic (*ependytes*) over his chiton. He is followed by an initiate, crowned, carrying a *bakchos*. In that part of the vase not shown here there follows a woman behind whom, according to Kourouniotes, is Persephone.

37.   Neck of water jar, black figures. Eleusis Museum, 1215. Kourouniotes: ᾿Εφημ. ᾿Αρχαιολ 1937. cit., pp. 223-253, figg. 12, 14, 17; Metzger: *Recherches* p. 28 no. 66. Our illustration shows the torch-bearer who leads the procession, bearing two torches, followed by a woman with a bunch (which however resembles in shape the torch of the torch-bearer); a man and a boy follow; on the other side is a somewhat similar scene.

38.   Spool, black figured, in the Nat. Museum of Athens, 501. From Eleusis. *Corpus Vasorum Antiquorum* 1, plate 5, 1-2.—Demeter offers a crown to Persephone, who holds a small branch; a procession of worshippers. Interpretation conjectural.

39.   *Pelike* (jar) from the Museo Naz. of Naples H 3358, Inv. no. 91083. Attic style, black figured. Poor quality design. Height 0.35 m. diam. of belly 0.280 m, 520-490 B.C. *Corpus Vasorum Antiquorum*, Naples III H e, p. 8 (bibl.), plate 13, 1-4 Italia 957; Metzger: *Recherches* p. 28, no. 64.—Side B. as described by CVA: 'to the right are seated side by side two cloaked women with fillets around their heads. They stretch out their hands towards a laden table which is set before them. To the left a bearded man wearing a cloak, with a fillet or band around his head, holds out a calyx bowl (*kylix*) in his left hand and in his right hand holds a goatskin bottle and a bunch of four twigs. Beside him is a Doric column, surmounted by a little turret room with open shutters; at the base of the capital can be seen purple brush strokes, the meaning of which is not clear. The man stretches out his hands and raises his head as if he were speaking. Beside the women, to the left, is a small tree and under the table a basket full of loaves. Between the women and the man is painted the word: MVSTA; incoherent signs are painted beside the man. Subject variously interpreted'. According to Pottier, it is a priest offering the mysteric drink (*kykeon*) to a couple of Eleusinian candidates for initiation (Daremberg-Saglio: *Dictionnaire des antiqu.*, II, fig. 2637). Metzger describes the scene rather differently: the seated figures are two youths, crowned with laurel. The tree is a myrtle. Inside the turret room, on a post, is a votive tablet with the two Dioscuri (according to Beazley). The goatskin bottle of the *telestès* (initiator) excludes the hypothesis of *kykeon*; the calyx-krater probably contains wine and the scene refers merely to a preliminary act of initiation, which would be still more in harmony with the secret character of the Mysteries. This difficulty led Jane Harrison: *Prolegomena* p. 156 and Beazley to recognise the rite of a *orpheotelestes*. The Eleusinian explanation is supported by the presence of the two Dioscuri in the votive tablet in the turret room above the column (see also no. 33).

40.   Eleusinian votive tablet. Found together with the *pinax* of Niinnion (no. 35). End of Vth century B.C. Original dimensions: height c. 0.60 m, width c. 1 m. A. Skias: 'Εφημ. 'Αρχαιολ. 1901, coll. 39-50 and plate 2; Metzger: *Recherches* p. 36 no. 15 plate XVI, I.—Demeter seated on a chest (or more probably a basket) covered with a cloth. To the left an *omphalos*, crowned, behind which stands Persephone. To the far left part of Pluton's cornucopia. To the right Iacchus and a wheel of the throne of Triptolemos, with a serpent.

41.   Triglyph of Pentelic marble. Part of the external ornamentation of the Little Metropolitan Church of Athens. C. Bötticher: *Der Altar des Eleusinion zu Athen, Philologus* 24, 1886, pp. 227-242 and plate at p. 230.—Symbols of the Eleusinian cult, on a marble which may have come from the Athenian Eleusinion. From the left on the triglyphs crossed bunches, poppy heads, *kerchnos* (cf. above, no. 35). On the metopes design of a patera (Mingazzini) and the skull of an ox.

42.   *Stele* in the Eleusis Museum. Pentelic marble; height 0.57 m, width 0.31 m. Possibly from the first half of the IVth century B.C. Mylonas: *Eleusis*, fig. 70.—Persephone as a

hydranos (water carrier) purifying a candidate for initiation? In her right hand she holds a *phiale*, or other similar receptacle.

43. Fragmentary statue of παῖς ἀφ'ἑστίας μυηθείς, found in Rome, during the excavation of the Quirinal Tunnel. *Bullettino Comunale* 1901, plate I, associated by Amelung with the Eleusinian cult (*Museums and Ruins of Rome*, I, p. 232. Concerning παῖς ἀφ'ἑστίας and his representations see Amelung: *Atti Pont. Accad. Rom. Archeol.* 1905, p. 115 et seqq. plates III, IV.); Katharine Esdaile: Ὁ ἀφ'ἑστίας *Journal of Hellenistic Studies*, 29, 1909, pp. 1-5, plate I a.—Figure of young initiate, especially chosen, as described in the formula rather doubtfully interpreted ἀφ'ἑστίας μυηθείς (for the purpose of special citizen representation in the initiatory rite?). Crowned with a band, he held the pig for the initiatory sacrifice (cf. no. 44); on the supporting tree trunk are a myrtle crown and a torch, the latter also adorned with fillets of myrtle, like a *bakchos*. Judging from no. 44 he must have worn one sandal only but in this case the other foot was shod (chthonic ritual, according to Amelung). A copy dating from the Augustan Age, a re-interpretation of a statuary type. Some aspects of the treatment of the chiton on the shoulders are reminiscent of the 'Eubuleus' type.

44. Another statue of παῖς ἀφ'ἑστίας (cf. no. 43). Palazzo dei Conservatori, Rome. Unknown origin. Restored. A much later type than no. 43, a copy of the Antonine Age. (For another copy of the head, in the Louvre, see Furtwängler: *Masterpieces* fig. 132; Reinach: *Têtes antiques*, plates XXIX and XXX, apparently a work of the middle of the Vth century B.C.).—Thick crown. One sandal, (see no. 43) and sacrificial pig.

45. Marble statuette. Eleusis Museum. IIIrd or IVth century B.C. A. Furtwängler: *Eleusinische Skulpturen, Athenische Mitteilungen* 20, 1895, p. 357 ad 1.—Wearing a sturdy crown, the boy holds the *bakchos* (see above no. 37) in his left hand; for remarks on the form of this bunch, which bears traces of red colour, see Rubensohn: *Athenische Mitteilungen*, 24, 1899, p. 57 et seq. n. 1. In his clenched right hand he may have held a pig. Certain aspects of this statuette remind Fürtwangler of the 'Eubuleus' type. See *Masterpieces*, London, 1895, p. 333 (above, no. 31 and, for the iconographical hypothesis of Furtwängler concerning 'Eubuleus' see above, no. 32; cf. also nos. 43 and 46). This Eleusinian statuette may also be compared with the same subject of nos. 43 and 44, that is with παῖς ἀφ'ἑστίας.

46. Lecythus-statuette, Attic, from Tanagra. Height 0.16 m. IVth century B.C. Fröhner: *Collection Eugène Piot*, Paris 1890, p. 42 et seq., no. 153; Furtwängler: *Masterpieces*, p. 332 et seq.—A youth with long curls, a tall diadem and a crown, holds a pig (Fröhner: a rabbit) and a bunch. According to Furtwängler not a worshipper but a god, the figure may be associated with the myth of Eubuleus. This opinion is open to discussion (see no. 45).

47. Sarcophagus from Torrenova. In Pentelic marble. Height 0.587 m, length 1.30 m, width 0.63 m., length of interior of coffin 1.07, presumably destined for a child. Some fragments of the upper part missing. According to Rizzo, derived from Greek types of the IVth century B.C. but with some signs of decadence. End of IInd or beginning of IIIrd

century A.D., perhaps from Asia Minor.—The relief of the principal side, here reproduced, is on two planes and the scene apparently derives from a painted, possible Hellenistic, original (not 'Alexandrine'). The whole action seems to represent a ceremony of mystical purification. The scene represented by the figures 2, 3 and 4 from the right is identical with that of no. 49, (terracotta relief in the Nat. Museum of Naples) while the figures 2 and 3 appear in another context in our nos. 50 and 51 (instead of Persephone with lowered torches a priestess who holds the cradle on the head of the veiled figure.) For an analysis of these differences and of the general meaning of these monuments, see the Introduction. We here give merely the list of characters from the right: Hecate (?), Dionysos (?), with leopard skin, torch and boots, who is pouring out a libation from a goblet, on the flame of an altar (rite called νηφάλια), together with the hierophant in characteristic attire, (the typical knot on his shoulders, and the knotted band round his head: see no. 48: Rizzo thinks he may be Eumolpos) and with a dish of fruit; a candidate for initiation, veiled, on a seat covered with a ram's skin (Διὸς κώδιον) with the head visible at his feet; Persephone with two torches pointing downwards, in the act of purifying the candidate and the ground below him. (Persephone, with lowered torches, is seen also on Athenian coins of the IInd century); Demeter, sceptred, is seated on a hamper which is covered with a cloth (Rizzo: fawn skin?); a snake is coiled around the hamper. She holds in her hand narcissi and hyacinths, instead of ears of corn and poppies. Other fragmentary figures (another *hierophantis*) on the second plane; than comes Iacchus, with torch and boots, but the style of his head and short chiton, and the way it is drawn about his neck, recall the type called 'Eubuleus'; cylindrical altar, crowned, with flame, fruits, pine cone and laurel bush. G.E. Rizzo: *Il sarcofago di Torrenova, Römische Mitteilungen*, 25, 1910, pp. 89-167, plate II.

48.   Detail of no. 47: head of hierophant. Rizzo: op. cit., pp. 156 et seqq. (*Excursus: Il costume del tipo artistico dello hierophantes*), plate V, no. 4.

49.   Relief in the Nat. Museum of Naples, *Museo Borbonico* V, plate 23; Ersilia Lovatelli Caetani: *Bullettino Commissione Archeol. Comunale di Roma*, 7, 1879, plate IV, 2; Rizzo: *Röm. Mitteil.* 25, cit. p. 104, fig. 5: it may be a fragment of a sarcophagus identical with that of Torrenova (no. 47; the restoration of the margin prevents examination).—Together these two form a first series of these initiation scenes. (Another series are characterised by the presence of the figure with a cradle, (the *liknon*), in place of the figure with lowered torches: see no. 47). The copper engraving in Winckelmann's *Monumenti inediti* II, plate 104; Lovatelli, op. cit. plate IV, 4, probably shows the same Neapolitan relief before restoration.

50.   Lovatelli urn. Rome, Museo Naz. delle Terme. From the burial ground of the freed slaves and servants of the *gens Statilia* near the Porta Maggiore. Cinerary urn of Greek marble, height 0.294 m, max. diam. 0.320 m, height of figures 0.220 m, from the beginning of the Imperial Age. It still contained remains of burnt bones: Ersilia Lovatelli Caetani: *Di un vaso cinerario con rappresentanze relative ai Misteri di Eleusi, Bullettino Commissione Archeol. Comunale di Roma* 7, 1879, pp. 5-18, plates I, II, III (and cf. for comparison, plates IV, V); Rizzo: *Röm. Mitteil.* 25, cit. plate VII from the cast); Helbig: *Führer*, II² 1168; P. Ducati: *Nota su alcuni monumenti relativi a divinità di Eleusi, Rendiconti Accad. Naz.*

dei Lincei, ser. V, vol. XVII, 1908, p. 375 et seqq. (bibl.).—It contains seven figures, arranged in three groups; the tripartite division, *qua* relating to three phases of an initiatory rite, is denied by Rizzo who observes that the figure to the left, leaning on a *bakchos* and not on a club, cannot be identified with Herakles who is represented in the last figure to the right, and whose initiation is portrayed in the three scenes of the complete representation. From the right: sacrifice of a pig by a candidate for initiation wearing a lion skin (?Herakles) whom Lovatelli also identifies in a figure of the Cumean hydria of the Hermitage (no. 5, with pig and club, but in a very different pose). Then come figures of a hierophant, of a veiled candidate, as in no. 47, and a woman who holds a sieve over the head of the latter, for purificatory purposes; a figure in front of Demeter stretches a hand towards the serpent's mouth, and finally Demeter, with three ears of corn on her head (an element from the Isis cult? see nos. 51 and 52) and a torch, followed by Persephone with her torch.

51.   Terracotta relief of the so-called Campana type. Rome, Museo Nazionale delle Terme. Moulded but retouched with scalpel, in two slabs; height 0.470 m, width respectively 0.55 and 0.350 m. Lovatelli: *Bull. Com.* 1879 cit., plate IV, I; Rizzo: *Röm. Mitteil.* 25, cit. p. 133 fig. 11, and plate VI.—Content similar to preceding; last figure to the right is missing.

52.   Detail of preceding.

53.   Fragments of Kabirian vase, with inscriptions. *Skyphos* (deep cup) from the excavations of the Kabirion of Thebes. Nat. Mus. of Athens, Inv. 10426. Dark figures on the yellow terracotta. Height 0.117 m; height of the smaller fragment 0.053 m. Style of painter of Kabiros (*terminus post quem*: 440 B.C.). P. Wolters and Gerda Bruns: *Das Kabirenheiligtum bei Theben*, I Bd., Berlin 1940, p. 96 and plate 5 and plate 44 fig. 1 and, for the inscriptions, p. 43, no. 53.—From the right: Kabiros (type of Dionysos) reclining on a couch, with a drinking cup. Crowned with ivy, he wears a knotted fillet. Before him is Pais (=the child) who serves him, taking the wine from a krater. To the left is Pratolaos, the First Man, a rather coarse and grotesque figure, like many of the human figures on these vases, and to the left, lower down than the two personages we have mentioned, Mitos (= the Sperm, which is mentioned in an Orphic text quoted by Clement of Alexandria—see Introduction) and Krateia (the 'Strong' woman), understood as the first progenitors. Mitos is also a grotesque figure, unlike Krateia who places her hand in a familiar manner on his shoulder. In the other fragment is another personage: Saty[ra ?]. The style was probably created for the Kabirian shrine; in some categories of these vases, according to most scholars, are represented parodies of myths and burlesque *dromena* (ritual actions) of the Kabirian cult, with some resemblance to the Phlyacic vases. In other vases we see possible reminiscences of dances of satyrs (Wolters-Bruns, p. 126 et seq.). For a remarkable scene of mythological-burlesque initiation (Hermes and a Pan, with other figures) see no. 55b.

54.   Fragment of a 'Kabirian vase'. *Skyphos* from the excavations of the Kabirion of Thebes. Nat. Mus. of Athens. Height of fragment: 0.109 m. Style of the 'painter of the Kabiros' (see no. 53).—Wolters-Bruns, op. cit., plate 8, fig. 1. Kabiros, crowned with olives, banqueting, with drinking cup and some traces of the painting of food. In front of the god is a pigeon.

55a.   Figured ornamentation of a Kabirian vase, Nat. Mus. of Athens, Inv. 427, style of 'painter of the *mystai*' (initiates), of a rather later date than nos. 53 and 54.—Wolters-Bruns: op. cit. p. 106, plate 33, fig. 3 and plate 53, fig. 3. From the right, two women cloaked up to the head, the second of whom holds the fillet of a candidate for initiation (cf. nos. 56 and 75). Then a grotesque personage, naked, with a large stomach, dancing, with torches, an initiate's fillet and two small branches on his head. There follow a personage crowned with small branches, bearing a cup and a pitcher and another with branches on his head and in his hand a 'pilgrim's staff'. Finally a figure wearing a chiton and cloak which completely covers head and forearm, with a crown and sprays of leaves on the veiled head (figure of candidate for initiation). For the explanation see no. 53, at end.

55b.   Fragmentary Kabirian vase. Gerda Bruns, *Archäologischer Anzeiger* 1967, pp. 268-270 and fig. 70.—Scene of mythological-burlesque 'initiation'. A bearded Hermes hands to a youth Pan the initiate's twigs and bands. Behind the Pan a woman whose head is partially veiled attends the ceremony. Other personages are singing and dancing.

56.   Figured ornamentation of a Kabirian vase, style of 'painter of the *mystai*' (see no. 55a). Berlin Museum, Inv. 3286. *Archäol. Anzeiger* 1895, p. 36, no. 30; 1937, col. 466 et seqq.; Wolters-Bruns, op. cit. plate 28, fig. 3.—Side B: from the left: a man seated on the end of a couch, with a typically knotted fillet and small branches on his head, seems to be imposing silence on another who is outstretched on the couch, attired in the same way; in front of the couch a table with a cup and food; to the right another couch with a seated person (with a knotted stick) and another reclining, similarly attired; in front, a similar table with a cup. See end of no. 53.

57.   Calyx-krater, style 'semi-grotesque Kabirian'. Akademisches Kunst-Museum, Bonn. Inv. 363. From Boeotia, end of Vth century B.C. (or rather beginnings of the IIIrd: Mingazzini). Height 0.20 m, diam. of the mouth 0.195 m. Annie D. Ure-P.N. Ure: *Boeotian Vases in the Ak. Kunstmus. Bonn, Archäol. Anzeiger* 1933, col. 29 et seqq. Wolters-Bruns, op. cit., plate 26, figs. 9 and 10.—Side A: Demeter with torches and small branches; an upright bough, rising from the ground, and long-necked marsh fowl. B: Iris with a *caduceus* (Kerényi: Hecate Angelos); a long necked bird with short claws. According to K. Kerényi, *Miti e misteri*, Turin, 1950, p. 170 et seqq., the birds seem to have a heavenly nature and so must have a mystical meaning, as have, by antithesis, the phallic characters, found very frequently in these vases.

58.   Kabiri of Samothrace. Rome, Lateran Mus. Marble from the so-called tomb of the Haterii, about 100 A.D. Benndorf-Schöne, *Antike Bildwerke des Lateranischen Museums* p. 236 et seqq., no. 359; R. Pettazzoni: *Ausonia* 3, 1908, pp. 79-90 (bibl.); Phyllis Williams Lehmann: *Samothrace. The Hieron*, Text I, Princeton 1969, pp. 325-327.—Four busts. From the right: Demeter with flaming torch and ears of corn, Jupiter (or Pluton?), Persephone, with fruits, a poppy and a garland, Hermes (missing but indicated by the caduceus) —that is, in Samothracian terms, οἱ μεγάλοι θεοί: Axieros, Axiokersos, Axiokersa, Kadmilos. The series of the gods is therefore complete, and consists of busts, reminiscent of a series of busts, also four in number, placed on the south fronton of the temple of Samothrace

in the second half of the IInd century B.C. One of these is identified by Phyllis Lehmann in the fragment of a female head, Samothrace Mus., 49.496 A (present height c. 0.155 m, width 0.28 m) found between the *hieron* (temple) and the so-called altar court (op. cit., p. 321, fig. 270), which apparently shows the same hair style and type of garments as the goddess of the Roman marble in question (another fragment p. 318, fig. 266).

59.   Fragments and reconstruction of the northern tympanon of the temple of Samothrace, IInd century B.C. Phyllis Williams Lehmann: *Samothrace; the Hieron*, Text I, Princeton 1969, figg. 211 and 212.—The interpretation of the figures is doubtful: Dike (or Themis?) with the Horai and the Moirai (?); the child Aetion.

60.   Terracotta votive tablet from Locri, somewhat archaic style, with traces of red colour. Between the end of the VIth century and 470-60 B.C. Height 0.20 m, max. width 0.27 m. Quagliati: *Ausonia*, 3, 1908, p. 154, fig. 18.—Scene of a woman ravished to the Underworld. She holds in her hand the votive cock, sacred to the Underworld gods, and containing an allusion to the hopes of the Nether World (at times the woman has an apple). Her ravisher may be a figure of Thanatos; still visible (according to the editor) is an elbow of Hermes. These scenes, in which we note that the dead person is always a female, are therefore partly connected with other tablets not representing a rape but a departure to Hades; in these the woman about to be drawn away has an expression not of dismay but of serenity (see no. 61). Some other scenes refer directly to the rape of Persephone: Quagliati, p. 168 et seqq. and fig. 24.

61.   Terracotta votive tablet from Locri (see no. 60). Max. height 20 1/2 cm, max. width 18 cm. Quagliati, op. cit., pp. 161-164 and fig. 21.—The grief of those who watch her departure (one has already turned away and another is bidding her farewell) contrast with the impassive calm of the dead woman (see also op. cit., p. 162, fig. 22).

62.   Terracotta votive tablet, Locri. Archaic style; from the beginning of the Vth century B.C.; height 0.25 m, width 0.22 m. Quagliati, op. cit., p. 175 et seqq., fig. 29 (cf. figs. 30 and 31).—Type of 'sacred conversation' frequently found in these *ex voto*. Typical is the back of the chair, in the form of a bird's long neck, which we find in other votive tablets (see below and nos. 64 and 65). The presence of the cock, (nos. 60, 63 and 64) and other indications such as the presence of Eros or of some other winged spirit, justify the association of these kinds of testimony with the concept of a world beyond the grave which we find in Magna Graecia (see also no. 67).—From the left: Pluton with bowl for libations and an apple, or pomegranate, Persephone, with a bowl (?) and a cock, Dionysos with a drinking cup. Above are bunches of grapes which draw attention to the presence, and importance, of this last mentioned god. As regards Persephone, with the cock or ears of corn, on a chair with a back shaped like a bird's long neck, see also Daremberg-Saglio, under *Proserpina*, fig. 5817 (see similar fragment in Quagliati, p. 174, fig. 28).

63.   Terracotta votive tablet, Locri. Height 0.20 m, width 0.21 1/2 m.—Before the door of Hades (?) is Persephone enthroned, with a bowl, Pluton with a drinking cup (an attribute assigned to Dionysos in no. 62) and, in front, Hermes with his winged sandals, carrying in

his arms a ram (bibl. Quagliati; for Hermes with a cock see Quagliati, p. 186 and fig. 39. Another deity appearing in these *ex voto* is Eros, p. 189, fig. 41).

64.   Fragment of a terracotta votive tablet. Locri. Max. height 0.10 m, max. width 0.12 m. Quagliati, op. cit., p. 144, fig. 4.—Persephone is seated on a throne which has a 'bird's neck' back (cf. no. 62) holding a wicker basket and a small box, attributes frequently found at Locri (no. 66) and in scenes of funeral rites on vases from Southern Italy (nos. 74 and 75).

65.   Terracotta votive tablet. Locri. Height 0.25 1/2 m, width c. 0.20 m. First decades of Vth century B.C. Quagliati, op. cit., p. 193 et seqq. and fig. 44, cf. 45.—Female figure seated on a throne with 'bird's neck' back (no. 62). She opens the lid of a hamper placed on a wooden chest of Ionian style (or rather a small table: Mingazzini). Inside of the hamper is an infant with long curls, an archaic figure, wrapped in a cloak. This is not an allusion to Erichthonios but probably to a mystic cult of a Dionysiac-Eleusinian type. Zuntz, *Persephone*, p. 168 thinks it impossible to identify the specific myth pictured in this scene, but identifies the woman as a Persephone; why not to think of a chthonic and 'mysteric' Dionysos, son of Persephone?

66.   Fragment of a votive tablet, with traces of red colour, 0.10 1/2 m x 0.10 1/2 m. Locri. Quagliati, op. cit., p. 144 et seq. and fig. 5.—To the left a coffer for objects of clothing (according to Mingazzini a little table with drawer), Quagliati; the reference is certainly of a sacral-mystical nature (cf. the position of the same piece of furniture in no. 64!), perhaps an attribute of Persephone enthroned (no. 64), to whom a human person offers a cock (not vice versa, as Quagliati asserts; in fact fig. 13 of Quagliati, p. 149 shows a dead warrior raising the sacred cock in his right hand). It is true that the same object is attributed to a man in fig. 12. Quagliati, p. 149.

67.   Terracottas with bust (*protome*) from Boeotia. IV and Vth centuries B.C. respectively Berlin, *Antiquarium*, 8163, 65 (height 0.23 m) and 8163, 63 (height 0.33 m); *Archäol. Anzeiger* 1888, p. 253 no. 4; F. Winter: *Die Typen der figürlichen Terrakotten*, I, p. 248, figs. 1 and 5.—In the upper tablet: female figure with cock (others too with an egg; or possibly with a dove, for ex. p. 250 nos. 1 and 2, or a pig, *ibid*., 7). In the lower tablet: Dionysos with an egg and a drinking cup (cf. 68). See also similar example Nilsson: *Dionysiac Mysteries* p. 119 fig. 33.

68.   Tarentine vase with Dionysiac and Mystery symbols: egg, cups and torches with bands, with grape motif ornamentation. Schauenburg: *Jahrbuch deutsch. archäol. Instituts* 68, 1953, p. 64 fig. 19.

69.   Apulian (or rather Tarentine, as the following ones) amphora, from Canosa. München 849. Furtwängler-Reichhold, *Griech. Vasenmalerei*, Serie I. plate X; *Vorlegeblätter für archäol. Übungen*, Series E, Vienna 1886, plate I; A. Winkler: *Die Darstellungen der Unterwelt auf unteritalischen Vasen*, Breslau 1888, p. 4 et seqq. (bibl.).—In the Underworld court is Hades with his sceptre tipped with an eagle, enthroned. The back of the throne is adorned with two Victories; he raises his hand in the direction of Persephone and

is in the act of speaking. Persephone has a torch with crossed sticks. Beside the two deities are the characteristic wheels. To the left of Persephone is Orpheus, from whose lyre hangs a band. But, contrary to the opinion of Winkler, here Orpheus is treated as a personage of the Mysteries, not as a hero leading Eurydike back (in spite of the Santangelo Amphora 709, *Vorlegeblätter*, series E, plate III, 2, where Orpheus is with Eurydike and Eros). In front of the royal court Herakles drives Cerberus out of Hades; Hermes shows him the way; in front of Cerberus is Hecate, the goddess of the Underworld. The object under the fore-paws of Cerberus is unidentified, but it resembles the funeral altar base in no. 77. To the left, below, is Sisyphus, pursued by a Fury, and to the right, below, is Tantalus. The orna-mentation below seems to allude to the meadows of the Underworld. Above Tantalus: three Underworld judges (cf. no. 71 with inscriptions): here we have the 'Asiatic' Minos, Aeacus (crowned with two sprays of corn) and Rhadamanthus. At the opposite end, behind Orpheus, are Dionysos (?) crowned with myrtle, Ariadne (?) and a son of them, with a toy, a little chariot (another example of these toys in Gerhard: *Apul. Vasenbilder*, plate XIV): the whole intended as a scene of an initiatory content. According to others these three personages represent a family of initiates. Above, to the left, Megara, the wife of Herakles whom he killed, and two of her children (cf. no. 71, and inscriptions) have bands (initia-tory?) round their heads and bandages around their bodies, covering wounds which seem to be bleeding (Winkler: the scene is therefore set in the Underworld) and other minor attributes; above them are two stars (to fill up space?). To the right are Dike with a sword, Peirithoos and Theseus (cf. no. 72, with inscriptions): therefore a scene of punishment in Hades.

70.   Apulian amphora, from Ruvo. Karlsruhe 388. *Vorlegeblätter* cit., Series E, plate II; Winkler: *Darstellungen* cit., p. 13 et seqq. (bibl.).—In the centre Pluton and Persephone, with Hecate who, bearing two torches, turns towards Orpheus who, according to Winkler, is interceding for Eurydike. From the left, above: Megara with the two Heraklides, without the attributes mentioned in no. 69. To the right, above, Peirithoos and Theseus, without Dike. Below are two Danaides (at least the one to the left is a Danaid). The youth beside them is probably Protesilaus who returns to the earth (Winkler). Behind Orpheus are two Furies, with their characteristic boots; one is seated on a panther skin, the other is winged. Below is Herakles dragging Cerberus who has a lion's body (and a dog's tail? in the vase no. 69 the tail is serpentine). Hermes is showing him the way. To the left: Sisyphus; to the right, below, another Hecate and another Danaid. It would be useless to attempt a specific comparison with the painting of Polygnotos in the Delphic Lesche.

71.   Apulian amphora, from Altamura. Naples Museum 3222. *Vorlegeblätter* cit., Series E, plate III; Winkler: *Darstellungen* cit., p. 18. Restored; remarkable for the inscriptions applied to most of the figures.—In the royal court of Hades Persephone gives a plate with fruit and two small branches to Pluton, who holds a cup (as in the Locri *pinax* no. 63) and a sceptre; to the left Orpheus and behind him two Furies, in typical costume (cf. no. 70), one of whom is seated on a panther skin (cf. no. 70). On the other's head is written [Π]OINAI which alludes to their specific function as Underworld daemon torturers of the damned (cf. no. 73). Above: Megara and the two Heraklides (inscription); a bandage on a wound similar to that of no. 69. To the right, above, are Pelops, Myrtilus and Hippodameia, iden-

tified by inscriptions. Below are the three judges, but Minos is replaced by Triptolemos (cf. no. 72). Above the stone of Sisyphus is a Fury (NAN: [M]AN[IA]? or [A]NAN [KH]?). To the right of Sisyphus are Hermes and Herakles in their traditional attitudes; there follows a female figure on a sea-horse (?), and then three Danaids, one of whom bears a dish with fruit.

72. Fragment of an Apulian amphora. Karlsruhe 258. *Vorlegeblätter* cit., Series E, plate VI, no. 3; Winkler: *Darstellungen* cit., p. 35, V.—Peirithoos and Dike (with a sword), identified by inscriptions; followed perhaps by Theseus (cf. nos. 69 and 70). Below are Triptolemos and Aiakos as judges of the Underworld (cf. no. 71).

73. From the Jatta amphora 1094. *Vorlegeblätter* cit. Series E, plate VI, no. 4; Winkler: *Darstellungen* cit., p. 57, IX.—Two damned souls, Peirithoos and Theseus, bound by a winged Fury, in front of Pluton and Persephone.

74. Apulian amphora. A. Genick-A. Furtwängler, *Griech. Keramik*² Berlin 1883, p. 18 and plate XVI.—Woman seated with a basket (cf. the Locri *pinax*, no. 64). To the right a crowned youth holds a bird (for which cf. also the scene Pagenstecher, *Unterital. Grabdenkm.*, plate III e, and plate VIa; cf. also our no. 77); to the left a female figure and a winged spirit who crowns the seated female figure. Probably a concentration of symbols of the privilege of an initiate in the world beyond (cf. 75, 76).

75. Apulian wine jar, Berlin. Genick-Furtwängler, *Griech. Keramik*² cit. plate XI.— Genre scene but apparently with references to initiation: basket, band, coffer. The basket and the bird seem to be attributes of the figure of a youth, inside a *heroon* (funeral shrine) with bands on each side, in Pagenstecher: *Unteritalische Grabdenkmäler*, plate III, e.

76. Lucanian amphora, Berlin. Genick-Furtwängler: *Griech. Keramik*² cit., only plate VIII-IX,—Perhaps a dead man considered as a hero. An armed figure holding a dish over his head. A bird is perched on the hero's leg and he holds a double twig. To the left another armed figure. Above, a sphere, crossed and pointed, frequently found in these figures and probably associated with initiations.

77. Apulian vase. Pagenstecher: *Unterital. Grabdenkmäler*, plate VIIc.—Funerary scenes with a concentration of iniation symbols. Youth upon an altar on which are also a krater and a pitcher. He holds a palm twig and a dove. To the left a youth with a crown and a dish; to the right a woman with a band and a basket. Below a lyre and a mirror. As regards the lyre, a personage who is playing such an instrument inside a *heroon* (to the left and right are two personages with a drooping band or fillet) is to be seen in Genick-Furtwängler: *Griech. Keramik*² cit. plate VI. Winkler, op. cit., p. 77 sees in an amphora in the British Museum (*Vorlegeblätter* cit. VI, 1) a scene of the offering of the lyre to the dead man (Elysian background). A basket with a band appears also in the vase reproduced Pagenstecher: *Unterital. Grabdenk.* plate III, a, and a somewhat similar basket covered with fruits (?) in the other funeral scene, idem, plate IV a.b. (but cf. Vb, VIc: short and open basket?).

78. Cylindrical marble base with basrelief. Whittall Collection, from the former Lansdowne Collection. Rizzo: *Thiasos. Bassorilievi greci di soggetto dionisiaco*, Rome, 1934, fig. 14. Pentelic marble. Height 0.55 m, diam. 0.38 m. Altar or base, with decorative elements common to late Hellenistic work and the Augustan Age.—On a plinth stands the 'statue' of Dionysos. The original composition, to which refer also the figures of Maenads in nos. 79 and 80, are no later than the last third of the Vth century B.C.

79. Basrelief with maenad and thyrsus. Rizzo: *Thiasos* cit. plate I. of unknown origin (Latium? Campania?). Pentelic marble. Height 1.405 m. actual width today 0.75 m. It appears also in other copies, less noteworthy; the original showed a troop of eight orgiastic Maenads (see no. 80) and dates from about the middle of the Vth century.

80. Basrelief with a maenad *chimairophonos* (goat-killer). From the Esquiline. Rome, Palazzo dei Conservatori. Rizzo: *Thiasos* cit. p. 11, fig. 5.

81. Jar with Dionysos περικιόνιος. Nat. Museum of Naples. Furtwängler-Reichhold: *Griech. Vasenmalerei*, series I, Text, Munich 1904, p. 193 et seq. and plate 36; Rizzo: *Thiasos* cit., p. 18 et seq. and fig. 8. O. Elia: *Lo stamnos dionisiaco di Nocera*, Apollo 3-4, 1963-64, pp. 79-92. Attic krater with a Dionysiac festival. End of the Periclean Age or a little later; it forms a single scene with the other side, where is grouped the god's *thiasos*.

82. Small pitcher used for the *choes* (Feast of Pitchers). Vlasto Collection. Athens G. Van Hoorn: *Choes and Anthesteria*, Leiden 1951, fig. 38, catal. no. 271, p. 97; M.P. Nilsson: *Dion. Myster.* p. 26, et seqq. and p. 27 fig. 4; Beazley: *Attic Red-figure-Vase Painters*[2] p. 1249, 13. From Anavysos (Attica), c. 430-425 B.C.—Mask of Dionysos in a cradle, which is decorated with sprigs of ivy. Nilsson agrees with Van Hoorn that the mask placed in the cradle was used for the ritualistic erection of the pole (for the [not-mysteric] festival of *Anthesteria*).

83. Reliefs of an Aretine goblet from the workshop of Marcus Perennius. Arezzo, Museo Civico. Rizzo: *Dionysos Mystes*, Società Reale di Napoli, *Memorie Reale Accad. di Archeol., Lettere e Belle Arti*, vol. III 1918 p. 39-102, p. 41, fig. 2 and p. 42; Nilsson: *Dionysiac Mysteries* p. 94, fig. 21. (Cast of an ancient original in G.H. Chase: *The Loeb Collection of Aretine Pottery*, New York 1908, p. 39 et seqq, plate I. To Metal models of Hellenistic Art.—In the centre a woman with a cradle; to the right, the sacrifice of a pig; to the left, a Silenus with the infant Dionysos. A nymph is garlanding an altar beside a column surmounted by a statuette of Priapus. Other Dionysiac figures. The connection is not clear. Possibly rites concerned with the first purification of Dionysos.

84. Small amphora, glass, found near Torrita, Val di Chiana. Mus. Arch. Naz. Florence. Ed. by E. Caetani-Lovatelli, *Atti R. Accad. Lincei* XII 1884 p. 591 et seqq. *Antichi Monum. Illustrati*, Roma 1889, plate XV; Rizzo: *Dionysos Mystes*, p. 56 et seq., p. 57, fig. 11; Nilsson: *Dionysiac Mysteries*, p. 82, fig. 14.—A child wearing a band and supporting on his head the cradle; many Dionysiac symbols; a *pedum* (shepherd's crook) with a ritual,

knotted band on the great mask of Silenus, or perhaps of Akratos (Paus. 1, 2, 5 and a vase painting with inscription: *Jo. Hell. St.* VII 55). Statuette of Priapus on a column adorned with a ritual band; a thyrsus in the form of a branch with an initiatory band held by the child initiate, veiled and holding on his head a covered cradle, without a phallus. (For this attitude of the boy see Rizzo, p. 44, fig. 5 and p. 59 fig. 13, respectively: front of sarcophagus in Munich, Glyptothek, and marble relief in the Louvre.)

85.   Terracotta in the Kestner Museum of Hanover. Campana: *Antiche opere in plastica,* plate 45; H. von Rohden-H. Winnefeld: *Architektonische Römische Tonreliefs der Kaiserzeit,* plates (Kekule: *Die ant. Terrakotten* vol. IV, 2), Berlin-Stuttgart 1911, plate 99; Rizzo: *Dionysos: Mystes,* cit., p. 58 fig. 12.—Veiled *mystes* Silenus with cradle and phallus, nymphs, of whom one has a kettledrum.

86.   Stucco from the Roman house of the Farnesina, Rostovzeff: *Mystic Italy,* p. 125, plate XXVI, I; Rizzo: *Dionysos Mystes,* p. 49 fig. 9; Nilsson: *Dion. Myst.,* p. 79, fig. 11.— A boy (Dionysos?) initiate. He has a thyrsus adorned with a band, boots (*embades*) and his head entirely covered with a veil. In front, Silenus is about to unveil the cradle which contains the phallus. Between the two nymphs a mystic basket.

87.   Painting from the Neronian Domus Aurea, from a copy by Francisco de Hollanda, in the Escurial codex 28, I, 20 fol. 13ᵛ and fol. 14. See Fr. Weege: *Das goldene Haus des Nero, Jahrb. deutsch. Archäol. Instit.* 28, 1913, p. 179 et seq., plate 9b; Rizzo: *Dionysos Mystes* fig. 10. Nilsson: *Dion. Myster.,* p. 85, fig. 16.—A young initiate, veiled, below a cradle with the phallus; a female figure rising from the earth, with a basket. This detail (for which cf. no. 86) suggests a mixture of Demetriac and Dionysiac ritual.

88.   Terracotta in the Louvre. Von Rohden-Winnefeld: *Archit. Röm. Tonreliefs* cit. plate 123, I (cf. the example in the Mus. Naz. delle Terme in Rome, Rizzo: *Dionysos Mystes* cit; p. 81 fig. 21).—'Aidos' (Modesty) fleeing before the revelation of the cradle (cf. in general Rizzo p. 82, n. 1 and Nilsson: *Dion. Myst.* pp. 23, 96, 114). A similar figure in the Cuicul mosaic, see H. Leschi: *Mos. à scènes dionysiaques de Djemila-Cuicul,* Monum. Piot 35, 1935-36, pp. 139 et seqq. and plates VIII and IX. In the centre of the Algerian mosaic, according to Leschi, is Orpheus and the fleeing woman in the same mosaic is Psyche (Nilsson does not agree) and she has traces of wings. These scenes remind us of the figure—although different—in no. 92. The problem is of the greatest importance.

89.   Terracotta in the British museum.—H. von Rohden and H. Winnefeld: *Archit. Röm. Tonreliefs,* plate 99; Rizzo: *Dionysos Mystes* p. 58; Nilsson: *Dionys. Myster.* p. 109 fig. 29. Infant Dionysos in the cradle carried by satyr with a thyrsus and a maenad with a torch.

90.   Great painting in the Villa dei Misteri, Pompei. Rizzo: *Dionysos Mystes* plate II, 1. End of Republican Age, first Augustan Age. It may derive from Greek originals of an earlier age, at the beginnings of Hellenistic art. It is worth noting, in the whole cycle, the absence of landscapes in the painting.—Child initiate, a woman who teaches him to read

the sacred formulae of the Mysteries: she may be *Teleté* or a priestess. For such books Rizzo quotes Paus. 8, 15, 2 in connection with books in the temple of the Eleusinian Demeter at Pheneus in Arcadia, where there were rites similar to those of Eleusis. He quotes also the inscription of Andania, Dittenberger: *Sylloge* II³ no. 736.

91.   Great painting from the Villa dei Misteri, another detail. Rizzo: *Dion. Mystes*, cit. plate III, lower part.—According to Rizzo, a chthonic Dionysos and Kore (Persephone of the Underworld) his mother. Instead the usual interpretation is that we have here Dionysos and Ariadne, symbols of the happiness of the initiates. To the left, a scene of divination of the lecanomancy type (?), with a Dionysiac mask. Dionysos has one sandal only (a reference to an initiatory rite? cf. no. 43, for Eleusis).

92.   Great painting from the Villa dei Misteri. Another deatail. Rizzo: *Dion. Mystes*, cit., p. 80 et seqq. and plate IV, 1 (upper part).—Unveiling of the cradle. A figure similar to a Fury (Ananke, Adrasteia) is using a whip (apparently against the kneeling woman to her right, not reproduced here). This 'Fury' is a figure of uncertain interpretation upon whom depends the significance of the whole cycle. In some way her attitude towards the cradle resembles that of the above mentioned Aidos in fig. 88 (and similar representations, ibid.); but the presence of the whip and the boots she is wearing, together with her severe aspect, remind one of the avenging Furies of the vases from Magna Graecia, who however are set in scenes from the Underworld (nos. 69 et seqq.).

93.   Apse of the 'basilica' of the Porta Maggiore, Rome. Bendinelli: *Il monumento sotterraneo di Porta Maggiore a Roma, Monumenti antichi dei Lincei*, 31, 1926, coll. 601-860, plate XI; Eugène Strong-Norah Jolliffer: *The stuccoes of the underground Basilica near the Porta Maggiore, Journal of Hellenistic Studies* 44, 1924, p. 103 et seqq.; J. Carcopino: *La basilique pythagoricienne de la Porte Majeure*, Paris 1926.—According to the most common interpretation, Sappho throws herself from the Leucadian rock in the direction of Phaon; she is urged on by Eros in the presence of Apollo. The interpretation of the figure depends very largely on the character assigned to the monument as a whole: possibly a meeting place for Neo-Pythagoreans (hence the primacy assigned to Apollo, but with references to scenes of the Dionysiac cult [no. 94] and the Dionysiac-Priapic ritual [no. 95]), or to sepulchral rites (which would explain equally well the presence of references to Mystery cults and the allusions to the blessedness of life in the Underworld, as in the central scene on the roof: the rape of Ganymede [Bendinelli: plate XVI]). According to Mingazzini, *Festschrift E. v. Mercklin*, Waldsassen 1964, pp. 90-105, the so-called basilica of the Porta Maggiore is to be interpreted as an *aestivus specus*, without special sacral significance.

94.   'Basilica' of Porta Maggiore. Bendinelli: op. cit., col. 375 fig. 24, cf. Strong-Jollifer, op. cit., p. 88.—Scene of sacred initiation with the cradle (two female personages: possibly a 'sacred conversation'?)

95.   'Basilica' of Porta Maggiore. Bendinelli: op. cit., plate XLI, 1, cf. Strong-Jollifer, op. cit., p. 96, fig. 16.—A sacred hall, to the left the statue of Priapus, supported; pilaster on a crowned base and a tree.

PLATES

PLATES

1. Demeter and Kore.

2. A child god and Athena.

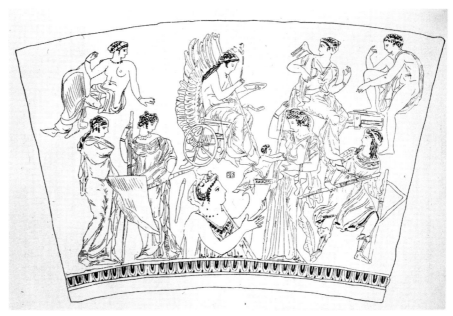

3. Demetriac scene.

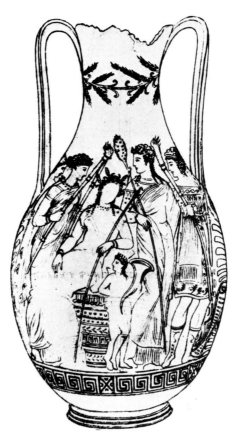

4. Demeter with Plutos.

5, 1. Triptolemos.

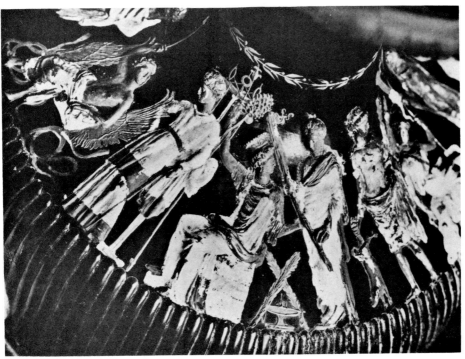

5, 2. Demeter and Dionysos.

5, 3. Herakles as an initiate.

6. Persephone between Demeter and Dionysos.

7. The same.

8. Demeter and the child Dionysos.

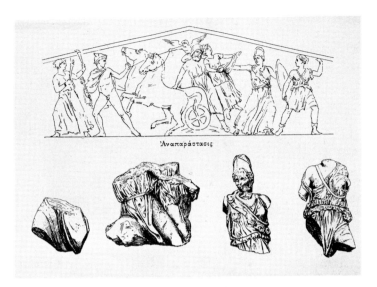

9. Rape of Persephone.

10. Rape of Persephone.

11. Return of Persephone.

12. Plutodotas.

13. Pluton and Persephone.

14. Hecate and Pluton.

15. Pluton and Demeter.

16. Pluton and Silenus.

17. Demeter, Persephone, Dionysos and Pluton (?).

19. Demeter and Persephone.

18. Dionysos-Bacchos and Demeter-Chloe.

22. Persephone on her mother's knees.

21. The same.

20. Demeter and Persephone (group).

23. Demeter and other mystery gods.

24. Mystery gods at a banquet.

25. Demeter, Triptolemos and other gods.

26. Mystery gods and worshippers.

27. Demeter, Triptolemos (?) and Persephone.

28. Demeter, Persephone and a child.

29. Demeter, Persephone and Asklepios with worshippers.

31. Eubuleus (?).

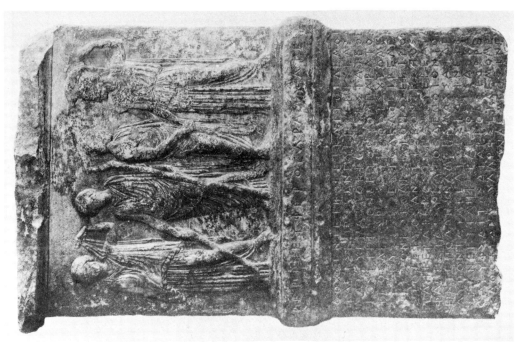

30. Mystery gods and inscription.

32. Eleusinian scene.

35. The Niinnion pinax.

33. Demeter with mythical initiates.

34. Hierophant between Iolaos and Herakles.

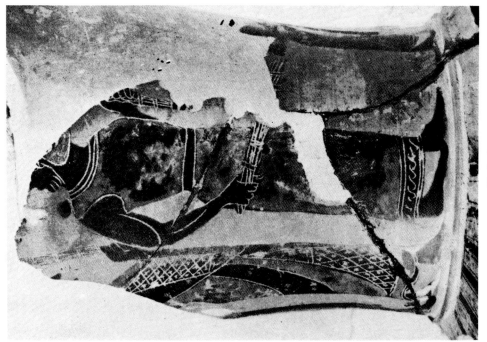

37. Daduchos.

36. Daduchos in procession.

38. Demeter offers a crown to Persephone.

40. Eleusinian votive tablet.

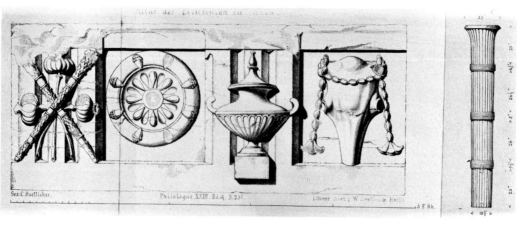

41. Symbols of the Eleusinian cult.

42. Persephone as hydranos.

43. Statue of initiate.

44. Statue of initiate.

45. Boy with the bakchos (ritual bunch).   46. Bunch and pig as ritual attributes.

47. Sarcophagus with mystery scenes.

48. Detail of 47: the head of the hierophant.

49. Relief with mystery scenes.

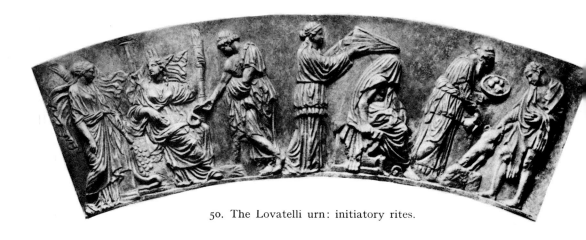

50. The Lovatelli urn: initiatory rites.

51. Initiatory rites.

52. Detail of 51.

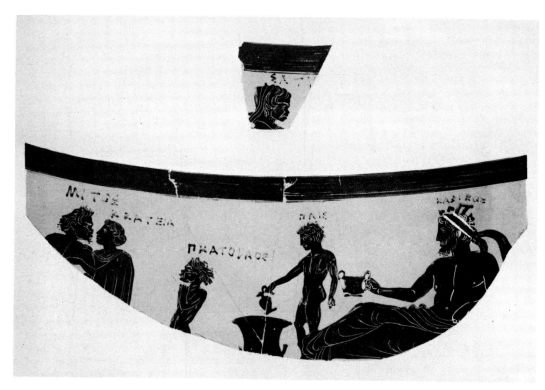

53. Fragments of a Kabirian vase.

54. Fragment of a Kabirian vase.

55a. Figured ornamentation of a Kabirian vase.

55b. Fragmentary Kabirian vase.

56. Figured ornamentation of a Kabirian vase.

57. Side A: Demeter. Side B: Iris.

58. Kabiri of Samothrace.

59. Fragments and reconstruction of the northern tympanon of the temple of Samothrace.

60. A woman ravished to the underworld.

61. Mourning women.

63. Persephone and other gods.

62. Type of 'sacred conversation'

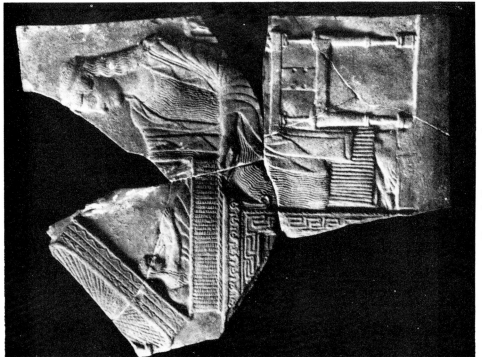

65. Female figure on a throne.

64. Persephone seated.

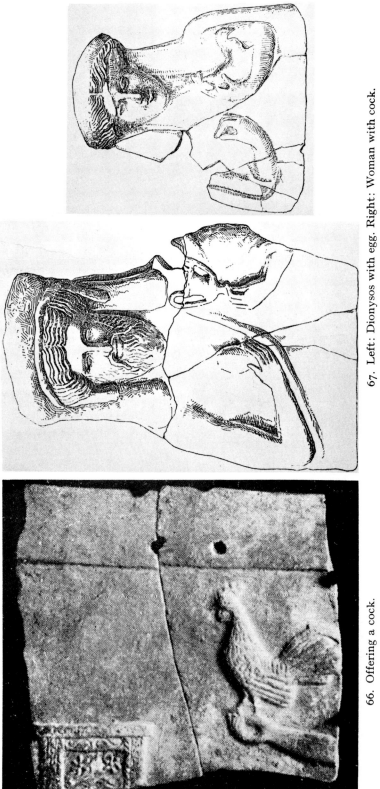

67. Left: Dionysos with egg. Right: Woman with cock.

66. Offering a cock.

68. Dionysiac and mystery symbols.

69. The underworld.

70. The underworld.

71. The underworld.

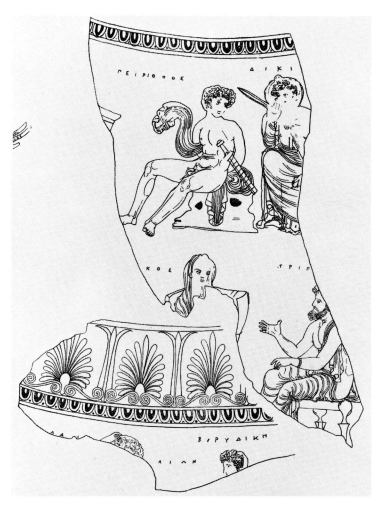

72. Underworld scene with Dike and judges.

73. Two damned souls bound by a winged fury.

75. Genre scene with references to initiation.

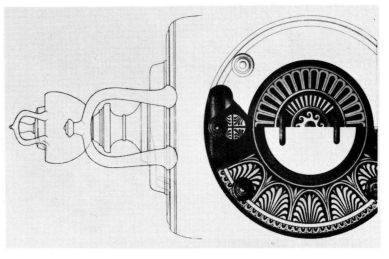

Symbols probably representing the privileges of an initiate in the world beyond.

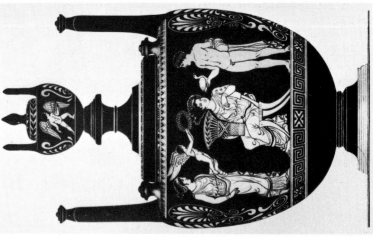

74. Symbols probably representing the privileges of an initiate in the world beyond.

77. Funerary scene with concentration of initiation symbols.

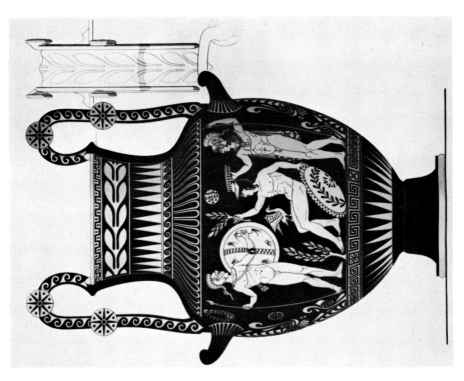

76. A dead man considered as a hero (?).

80. Maenad goat-killer.

79. Maenad.

78. 'Statue' of Dionysos.

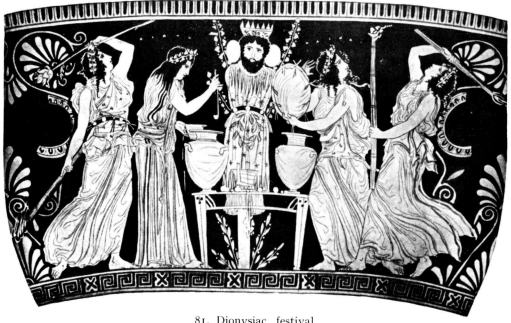

81. Dionysiac festival.

82. Mask of Dionysos in a cradle.

83. Mystery scenes.

84. A child initiate and Dionysiac symbols.

85. Initiate, Silenus and nymphs.

86. Mystery scene.

88. Modesty (Aidos) fleeing before the revelation of the cradle.

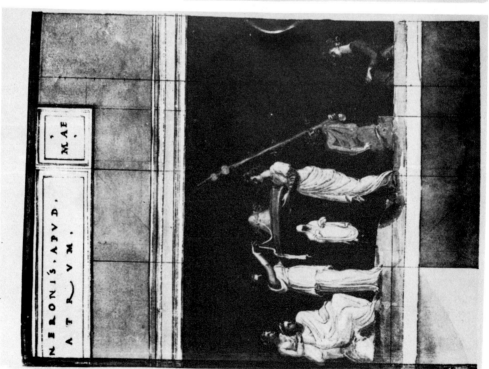

87. Mystery scene.

89. The cradle carried by a satyr.

90. The teaching of a child initiate.

91. Mystery scene.

92. Mystery scene.

93. The Leukadian rock (?).

94. Initiation scene.

95. Priapus.